DISABLING
AMERICA

DISABLING AMERICA

THE UNINTENDED CONSEQUENCES
OF GOVERNMENT'S
PROTECTION OF THE HANDICAPPED

GREG PERRY

WND BOOKS

Nashville

www.WNDBooks.com

Published in Nashville, Tennessee, by WND Books.

Library of Congress Cataloging-in-Publication Data

Perry, Greg M.
    Disabling America : the unintended consequences of government's protection of the handicapped / Greg Perry.
    p. cm.
    ISBN 0-7852-6225-3
    Includes bibliographical references and index.
    1. People with disabilities—Government policy—United States. 2. People with disabilities—Legal status, laws, etc.—United States. 3. United States. Americans with Disabilities Act of 1990. I. Title.
    HV1553.P463 2003
    362.4'0973—dc22

2003021959

Printed in the United States of America

03 04 05 06 07 BVG 5 4 3 2 1

CONTENTS

Introduction

Do you run a small business? Enjoy going to movies and restaurants? Don't like paying higher prices for the goods you buy or services you use?

Whether you know it or not, the Americans with Disabilities Act is making life hard for you—regardless of whether you're actually disabled. In fact, if you are *not* disabled you may have no idea how badly the ADA actually impacts your life in higher costs, hamstringing regulations, invasive bureaucracies, frivolous lawsuits, and so much more. *Disabling America* is here to disabuse you, to show you how the ADA in the guise of compassion for the handicapped actually harms more than helps.

While this book deals with the effects of government policy gone wrong, it is really about you—the day-to-day person affected by the ADA. As such, I've avoided writing *Disabling America* like a policy book. Instead, I've written on a more personal level. I've included abundant real-world examples and omitted meaningless charts, graphs, and tedious government statistics found in so many writings related to governmental policy.

As for myself, I am so very grateful that I was born long before the ADA was put into law. Under its auspices, I believe that I would be a failure instead of what most would consider a success. While *Disabling America* is certainly not about me, the fact that I was born handicapped, coupled with the fact that I have been following the ramifications of this law since its inception, puts me in a prime position to analyze the ADA for both the good and bad results it may produce. If I did not bring my own life into book and how the ADA has helped or hindered me, then this book would not be a fair or complete witness. Thus, I have attempted to weave my firsthand accounts and concerns about the ADA throughout.

Most Americans are extremely unfamiliar with the Americans with Disabilities Act. They might see the ADA as something that helps those who need extra help. What they do not know is that the ADA has infiltrated all Americans' lives in ways that you will be shocked to learn. The businesses you enter, the prices you pay, the design of products you buy, the Web sites you visit, and the very home and neighborhood you live in have already been changed by the ADA.

The length of the ADA's tentacles is even more astonishing when one considers its short history—the ADA is only fifteen years old.

Disabling America holds many surprises. The law's ugly and unintended consequences abound. In each chapter, I strive to present the ADA's effect on America and on the world accurately.

Chapter One, "Compassion or Coercion," gives you the overview needed to understand what the ADA is actually about. You will immediately begin to question whether the ADA helps those it's supposed to help or intrusively harms them and others in unexpected ways.

Chapter Two, "ADA: 'Abuses Do Abound,'" recounts massive fraud and deceit linked to the ADA. The ADA's history has been plagued with massive questionable lawsuits where able-bodied individuals seem to seek high profits in the ADA.

Chapter Three, "Confessions of a Handicapped Man," describes what my life has been like before and after the Americans with Disabilities Act was signed law. Growing up in a pre-ADA world gave me the chance to succeed whereas I would question my success if I'd been born with my same handicaps a few ADA-enhanced years later.

Chapter Four, "Good Intentions and Unintended Consequences," is the first time you glimpse the behind-the-scenes manipulation that went into passing the ADA. Given that the handicapped were employed and did not see themselves as victims, the disability advocates who profit from the ADA appear to have set out to create an America full of discrimination and hatred towards this group of people.

Chapter Five, "Spreading the Burden: The ADA in the Workplace," describes how you as a customer and you as an employee suffer due to the ADA. It's not just the large businesses that are hit; quite the contrary. The small businesses pay the largest cost percentage in the ADA's unending search for money and control of the workplace.

Chapter Six, "Social Unrest and the ADA," is one of the most eye-opening of all the chapters in *Disabling America*. Are ADA advocates truly concerned with the most innocent and most helpless of the disabled? This chapter presents clear proof that these advocates willingly look the other way when the most helpless of America's disabled are harmed.

Chapter Seven, "Children and Disabled Education," continues to show how disability advocates are growing in numbers. To justify their existence, they must create more and more disabled "victims." One major problem is that those people become victims of the ADA itself. The biggest problem, however, is that those victims are often your very own children.

Chapter Eight, "The ADA vs. The Free Market," pits two foes against each other: the free marketplace and the Americans with Disabilities Act. The free marketplace flourishes under freedom while the ADA flourishes under draconian rules, regulations, fines, and lawsuits.

Chapter Nine, "The ADA Around the World," describes how America's lawmakers—the very ones who increased discrimination and troubles for the handicapped after passing the ADA—now export that failure to disabled people around the world. Sadly we now see new worldwide problems generated in the guise of compassion.

Chapter Ten, "Your Future with the ADA," looks out a few years to see where today's ADA is taking us. If we follow the current course, we have only just begun to see the dramatic impact the ADA regulators have on our lives. (They are coming into your home soon, so keep your doors locked.)

Also, for your reading pleasure (or horror), I've included an appendix containing excerpts from the Americans with Disabilities Act and related federal disability legislation.

I do not intend here to hurt the handicapped by exposing the ADA's details and consequences—quite the opposite. While I believe that the ADA is already far too embedded in America to ever be entirely removed, it's my hope that exposure and disclosure of the ADA's consequences will keep the ADA and its puppeteers from gaining a greater controlling stronghold in Americans' lives.

This book would hardly be possible without Joseph Farah, cofounder of WND Books and editor and CEO of WorldNetDaily.com, who knew this book needed to be written. Perhaps as much of my thanks should also go to Joel Miller who turned the draft I submitted into a readable book. The rest of the wonderful people at WorldNetDaily.com and WND Books, who work tirelessly to bring you truth, made it possible to put this book into your hands. I am eternally grateful to them all.

GREG PERRY
Tulsa, Oklahoma
Greg@SimpleRentHouses.com

1

COMPASSION OR COERCION

An elderly lady struggles with her wheelchair to cross a busy Manhattan avenue. Moving alongside her you say that you are crossing also and together you can both cross safely. She lets you guide her as the two of you maneuver across the thoroughfare.

Now consider another scenario: A government official first sees the elderly lady approach the crosswalk, points a gun at you, and demands that you help the lady across the street.

One is an act of compassion, and one is an act of coercion. Coercion can never produce compassion.

I n 1990, President George H. W. Bush signed the Americans with Disabilities Act into law. The law was strongly encouraged by fellow Republican Senator Bob Dole, who had taken a prompt interest in the ADA from its inception perhaps due to the injury he sustained in World War II.

In his final speech to the Senate in 1995, Dole proudly announced that the Americans with Disabilities Act was one of his three proudest accomplishments while serving in the Senate. The only accomplishment he listed as being more important to his career than the ADA was strengthening the United States Food Stamp Program. TurnLeft.com listed the ADA as a "rare nod in favor of liberalism by Mr. Dole." In retrospect, some conservatives have brought into question the site's use of the term *rare*.

As declared on the ADA's Web site, ADA.gov, the Americans with Disabilities Act is intended "To give civil rights protections to individuals with disabilities similar to those provided to individuals on the basis of race, color, sex, national origin, age, and religion. It guarantees equal opportunity for individuals with disabilities in public accommodations, employment, transportation, state and local government services, and telecommunications."[1] That's the intention, sure enough, but the unintended consequences of the law and its many abuses guarantee the intention is not the reality. The ADA infiltrates the lives of average Americans in ways far beyond what we usually think—wheelchair signs in parking lots and grab bars in public restrooms—but most do not know its full effects.

Once you see how the Americans with Disabilities Act really and fully affects both disabled and non-disabled alike, you then can gauge the effectiveness of this much-vaunted law and determine if the means justify—or even comes close to achieving—its stated goals.

CARING BY GUNPOINT

Before venturing further, please remember that the Americans with Disabilities Act is a *law*. If one violates this law, the best one can expect is a lawsuit and possibly an arrest depending on how egregiously its requirements are ignored.

Considering its goals, you might expect the Americans with Disabilities Act to be regulated by the Department of Health and Human Services. Actually, while the HHS has some control over the ADA's administration, the ADA falls directly under the United States Department of Justice. ADA.gov greets its visitors with the official seal of the DOJ, and if you call the ADA information line, you are calling the official "United States Department of Justice ADA Information Line." For eight years, Attorney General Janet Reno had responsibility for the enforcement of the ADA.

The U.S. government takes the ADA very seriously indeed.

Please note that law enforcement *should* be the primary responsibility of the Department of Justice. Nothing is inherently wrong when a law falls within its jurisdiction—quite the contrary. Many people believe that too many unofficial laws known as *regulations* (or as critics call them, *unconstitutional laws*) fall into the hands of too many non-DOJ officials. They say that layers of bureaucrats control a plethora of environmental, taxation, health, and other regulations that are not called "laws" and therefore not monitored appropriately and ultimately by the Department of Justice. If a law is good, it should ultimately be enforced by the Department of Justice.

But *Disabling America* questions whether or not the ADA should ever have been made into law in the first place. Does the government really have the ability and the authority to regulate the public's reaction to disabilities? Both ability and authority are needed for a law to be good so it can protect and serve the people it proposes to help. In the guise of compassion, we get state coercion. With a legal gun to your head, the government now states that you will be compassionate to the disabled and you must implement that compassion exactly the way the government spells out that you are to do so. Such force is cruel to both the disabled and the non-disabled. Compassion comes from the heart, never from the state.

THE ADA: IT'S YOUR MONEY

Why should the general public learn or care about the ADA? Why should healthy people hear its history, be it positive or negative? Do the ADA's unintended consequences overshadow its good, and should the public be concerned? Why should you learn what the ADA is all about if no one in your family has need of this law?

The primary answer is that you are paying for the ADA. You pay for the ADA's administration, you pay for the ADA's publications, you pay to bring about the ADA's lawsuits against businesses and organizations, you pay the damages of those businesses and organizations as customers, you pay for the ADA officials' salaries, and you pay higher prices virtually everywhere you go thanks to the ADA. If the ADA is a good law, then the costs should be worth the result. If, on the other hand, it is not a good law, the costs should be exposed for what they are—legalized theft.

MORE EQUAL THAN OTHERS?

The Americans with Disabilities Act has been called "Civil Rights for the Disabled."[2] This assumes that disabled American citizens have been widely discriminated against. But you have to look long and hard to find where these citizens had crutches kicked out from under their arms before the ADA was implemented. The ADA is purported to give disabled citizens equal access, equal accommodation, and equal protection under the law.

The proponents of the ADA, for instance, fought hard so that those with parking permits had equal access in parking lots. In other words, the disabled have extra-wide parking spaces right next to building entrances which are available no matter how full the non-disabled spaces become. The disabled spaces must measure at least eight-feet wide, designated with the international wheelchair symbol, and be van-accessible. Vertical clearance of more than eight feet on the vehicular route into the space must be at least ninety-eight inches also on the route to the space and along the route to an exit.[3] (One must give the authors of ADA law credit for being extra specific and verbose.) So where is the "equal" in "equal access"?

In a brochure written for business owners, the ADA states, "It is illegal to segregate people with disabilities in one area by designating it as an accessible area to be used only by people with disabilities."[4] By these words, no accessible area can be segregated solely for use by the disabled. You can test how little the ADA's authors mean this by trying to park in a handicapped parking space without a permit. Such a statement should raise concern as it suggests that no area can be designated as a handicapped area because doing so would segregate (and separate) the disabled. Yet virtually every aspect of the Americans with Disabilities Act does just that. The ADA's entire massive collection of rules and regulations states how areas must be changed, marked, and separated for those with disabilities. The very specifications of the ADA violate its own statement against segregation.

ADA opponents also ask how equal the ADA-approved door opening widths are. Can all disabled citizens now get through the required thirty-two-inch-or-greater width? The answer is a resounding "No." Bed-ridden patients could never be wheeled through such a small opening. So equal access actually means equal for some disabled but not for all disabled. Perhaps some ADA opponents won't like that fact being mentioned out of a very real fear that the Department of Justice might update the minimum door width requirements to handle bed widths soon—I don't want to give the DOJ any more ways to intimidate.

Without wanting to get too tongue-in-cheek about the law, let it be said that many *good intentions* paved the road to the ADA.

WHO NEEDS IT?

Nobody wants to see disabled people harmed. Nobody wants to see disabled people left out of life-fulfilling activities. Yet I will attempt to show that the ADA causes more harm than good. That harm often goes undetected below our radars. Unseen harm is far more damaging to a society than visible harm because well-meaning people cannot address problems if they do not know or see that the problems are there.

Speaking as someone who, without doubt, would be considered handicapped compared to an assumed average man (for details see Chapter Three), let me state plainly that discrimination has certainly run rampant in America's past and at times still does for many. We're all guilty of this charge at some point in our lives. Nevertheless, there is very little evidence for a true pattern of discrimination against the handicapped in our history. While anecdotal, single-case evidence may sometimes prove differently (and I am sure I will hear such anecdotal evidence in ample supply when this book hits the shelves), you cannot prove a general case with a specific. This book strives to show that this all-encompassing, world-changing law solely based on anecdotal evidence creates far more discrimination than it prevents.

Obviously, one of the ADA's primary goals at its inception was to protect the handicapped from discrimination. The effect of the law is quite the opposite. My charge in a nutshell: the ADA actually nurtures discrimination against the handicapped.

YOU DON'T GET WHAT YOU PAY FOR

Please consider a pre-ADA business owner of a new, small coffee shop. The owner is struggling to make ends meet because a startup business rarely generates sufficient cash flow and loans are difficult to obtain. In such a hypothetical scenario, the owner probably works in the shop more hours than any other employee. There is no doubt that the owner values each and every customer's business.

Suppose such an owner sees a man pushing a walker approach the front door. Hardly an American business owner exists who would not happily stop immediately to go help the person with the door, ask if there is any assistance at all needed while in the shop, leave the "Order Here" area to bring a menu, take the order, and serve coffee and re-fills to whatever table at which the disabled customer wants to sit.

Consider that same business owner in a post-ADA America. He was given two or three years in the mid-1990s to spend from $20,000 to well over $75,000 to change the entire parking lot layout, to widen every door, to change all door knobs (round doorknobs are illegal in post-ADA commercial America—you didn't know that, did you?), to lower some counters, to raise other counters, to add a ramp in front, to change the bathroom entrance, to replace every bathroom fixture, to add handles and bars throughout, to replace some built-in benches and stools, to eliminate inventory so as to have room to widen the aisles, and possibly be required to provide home delivery. All of these cause financial hardship for such a small business.

You now need to ask yourself the real question: Is that small business owner *more* likely or *less* likely to view disabled customers with happiness, care, and compassion?

Now that the government has forced the owner to spend so much money to renovate the doors, possibly requiring one employee to be let go—often a relative in such a small shop—he is *far less likely* to go the extra mile to help disabled customers. Instead, the owner is more likely to let the handicapped customer fend for herself because the owner was already forced to accommodate that customer under threat of losing his business for not complying with ADA-required changes. His help has already been coerced; he's not likely to offer more.

History proves time and time again that when the government provides a service to a select group of people, families and friends and caring strangers stop helping. When the government gives thousands of welfare dollars in food, housing, clothing, and other living expenses to a household, extended family members almost always stop helping, and simultaneously a breakdown in traditional family structures begins to occur. Marvin Olasky explains this phenomenon well when he describes the American welfare system, which is generous with money but stingy on human involvement. People used to want to help others, but now they want to help by dispensing government money (after the government keeps its transaction fee).[5]

You see this phenomenon in all aspects of governmental control and redistribution of wealth. When the government takes over education and childcare, parents relinquish their own responsibility. Consider when the government takes money to build museums from people who don't want to visit museums so that people who want to go to museums get in free. Those who want the museums should be the ones paying the bills, but the very opposite takes place. Certainly some private money pays for museums, but the public "endowments" come right out of the pocketbooks of many who care nothing for them. When the government punishes criminals with community service work such as cleaning alongside roads and highways, the public is less likely to pick up its own litter. (Only government would think it is good to train the public that a nice idea such as community service should be turned into a punishment.) When the government takes over a free society's traditional responsibilities, that now less-free society instantly begins to abandon its natural instinct to help those who need and want help.

So who can blame the business owner who believes enough has been done to accommodate the disabled and no longer feels compelled to come to the aid of a handicapped man or woman who approaches the business's ADA-required new $4,000 door and frame? The ADA required equal treatment, and the ADA got equal treatment; handicapped customers can now fend for themselves just as everybody else does. Compassion and good deeds have been turned into forced coercion by the government. Now discrimination can safely rear its ugly head and go completely unnoticed because the ADA's *i*'s are dotted and its *t*'s are crossed.

WE'RE ALL "DISABLED" NOW

Dissent against the ADA is rare. A number of explanations are obvious. Many hesitate to discuss the ADA negatively for fear of being seen as anti-handicapped. The current hands-off-the-ADA attitude seems to be more a civil rights issue for the ADA itself than civil rights for the disabled. In other words, the ADA needs to be defended and protected more than handicapped people themselves. ADA advocates certainly will respond to this book as a biased and unnecessary portrayal of the ADA's negative consequences. They will ask, "How can such a negative message be helpful when the Americans with Disabilities Act provides so many needed services for so many needy disabled persons?"

Attorneys involved in ADA cases and others who share in massive financial gains provided by such a law might question my criticism of the ADA. However, Arkansas Judge H. Franklin Waters states that the ADA has the effect of "turning federal courts into a workers' compensation commission" and allowing almost anything to be called a "disability" and therefore worthy of federal protection.[6]

Judge Waters has insight. He understands why the term "handicapped" has virtually been removed from our politically-correct vocabulary and replaced with the more general "disabled." Proving that one is disabled is easier than proving that one is handicapped. Consider Waters' account of the dentist fired for fondling patients; he says that the dentist used as a defense that his urges were innocently the result of a "disability." The case would sound more ludicrous, if that is possible, had the dentist claimed that his urges were because he was "handicapped."

Words have meaning. If words did not move people to think and act in certain desired directions, then the major publishing houses of the world would have no income. Madison Avenue would not be awash in billions of dollars annually developing phrases and jingles to sell products. Vague euphemisms such as *disabled*, *access*, and *accommodation* constantly work to orchestrate a positive spin for the ADA. These unspecific words allow much to happen under the auspices of helping those in need. Chapter Two, "ADA: 'Abuses Do Abound,'" recounts numerous examples of how the ADA has been the tool for winning trials and getting people what they want. On a subjective note, for some reason the term of choice for most ADA advocates is *disabled persons* instead of *disabled people*. To me, this turns these real people into name-less, faceless, generic "persons." I doubt it is the ADA advocates' inten-tion to do this, and yet the more personal *disabled people* and the more accurate *handicapped people* attach a truer meaning to the folks whose lives are being monitored and changed at the altar of good intentions.

While penning this section, I ran across an article that described the annual "Day of Silence."[7] Nearly two thousand colleges, high schools, and middle schools across the country participate in this day that has been promoted and paid for by students' parents and neighbors' taxes for almost a decade. The day is said to be a movement to support gay, lesbian, bisexual, and transgender people who have purportedly been unable to speak freely about who they are and what they really want to do. It will be interesting to see if such a group is formed by these schools for the "deafening silence" that has rarely been breached by speaking out against the Americans with Disabilities Act. Will the First Amendment attorneys and free-speech boosters come to the aid of this title when it is attacked?

THE NUMBERS RACKET

The ADA's designers seem to prefer the law's ambiguity. The Cato Institute reveals that ADA proponents originally claimed that 43 million out of the total 260 million Americans are disabled. That number would comprise more than 16 percent of the population. Edward L. Hudgins, writing for Cato's *Regulation* magazine, discloses that only 2.8 million people are blind, deaf, and wheelchair-bound—the groups generally thought of by the public when they hear that the Americans with Disabilities Act protects the disabled.[8] In addition, it was from this small percentage of people who were the ones shown and discussed publicly during debates that surrounded the ADA's origin. What if the ADA only accommodated those truly handicapped 2.8 million Americans instead of the 43 million they say existed? Then the ADA would only be adding to the discrimination against those 2.8 million Americans instead of the larger group of 43 million—that is little comfort. Hudgins explains that the other 40 million which the ADA assumes to be disabled are comprised of *everybody* over 65 years old, as well as those with mental disorders and emotional problems. Severe mental problems are rightly termed as handicaps. But to include emotional problems opens the door to the ADA's "legal wrecking ball," as Craig E. Richardson and Geoff C. Ziebart so aptly name it due to the rampant fraudulent claims that can now be made by anyone.[9]

There were more than 31 million people who were over sixty-five when the ADA created these disabled estimates. Do the math. Over 72 percent of people "used" (I didn't choose that term lightly) to arrive at the number of American disabled were labeled as disabled only because they were born before 1925. I'd say folks who have lived that long are the opposite of disabled; they show a strong *ability* to survive in the face of severe times such as wars and a devastating economic depression. More important, such an inclusion of over-sixty-five-year-olds is an offense to the majority of those people who have no need and no desire to be considered disabled.

This inflation of numbers during debates that got the law passed causes even more concern considering what took place just three years after the signing. In August of 1993, the EEOC announced that obesity should be regarded as a protected disability under the Americans with Disabilities Act, thereby placing potentially tens of millions of additional people beneath the ADA's umbrella.[10]

HOW DANGEROUS IS THIS BOOK?

Is writing against the ADA a slight to handicapped people? Does exposure to the ADA's rampant abuses harm those the Americans with Disabilities Act purports to help?

I have been accused of wanting to hurt those who might benefit from the ADA. This is highly ironic considering my physical situation. After reading Chapter Three where you learn about my life and how the ADA might have affected me, I doubt you will believe I want disabled folks to be harmed in any way.

If I wanted to harm the handicapped, I wouldn't write a book. I would give far more funding to the ADA and petition Congress to strengthen the ADA's requirements and penalties. Without question, one of the most troublesome aspects of the ADA is that the subject is rarely discussed in spite of the harm that it may be doing. When one hears an ADA discussion on a radio show or reads an article in print, the story presupposes that the ADA is a good thing and that people are helped by it and that society benefits from it. The entire assumption seems to be how to use, implement, and expand the ADA even further.

A few years ago, I approached a major publishing house with the idea for this book. They would not touch the topic, I surmise due to fear of looking as though they were against handicapped people getting the help they need. Fortunately for me, more abuses have surfaced in the interim to write about, and fortunately for you, the reader, WND Books agreed to publish *Disabling America*.

THE UNNECESSARY ADA

Some conservatives say that the Americans with Disabilities Act is unneeded because America already has a civil rights law in place. They say that all are equal under the law and that discrimination against any individual for any reason is covered already.

Consider the St. Louis jury that awarded $6,000 to a suburban woman who got a bad hairdo.[11] Without any help from the ADA as far as can be determined from the news reports, a Creve Coeur, Missouri, woman accused a local hair studio of causing her hair to fall out. She said that as more and more clumps of hair fell out, she went into a severe enough depression that she ultimately had to retire early from a teaching position at the local university. Any ADA trial lawyer worth his percentage of awarded damages would quickly suggest that her depression equals a disability. A quick survey of routine ADA damage award amounts shows that she would have won far more than her $6,000 if she had sued under the ADA.

When you see past the ADA's veiled and sometimes well-intended attempt to help the disabled, you find that the ADA causes far more damage than it provides help to the handicapped.

THE FREE-MARKET PROVISION

Throughout this book, I try to give full coverage to anything positive about the ADA. A warning is in order, however: the ADA has its tentacular hold on virtually every element of American society. The negative ramifications of its influence are growing exponentially, especially for those it purports to help most. The free market, however, is another story.

In spite of the immovable wall of ADA proponents, publications, and trial lawyers, the free market has the tools to provide any assistance that handicapped people need. This book was never intended to be a cynical tirade against the ADA. Not completely, that is, because you can't fight something with nothing, and if the ADA is wrong then a better solution should be provided. You will learn how the free market has stepped in time and time again to provide services, support, and physical aid for the handicapped. What's more, the free market mechanism has built-in instincts that filter out "false positives"—those pseudo-disabled who attempt to take advantage of the benefits.

Consider a couple of large department stores in an ADA-free world, next door to each other in the same mall. One store decides, for whatever reason, not to install handicapped facilities throughout the store. The other does make the changes. The altered store will benefit from handicapped people's business. And yet, consider if only one or two people in that entire community were actually handicapped. Perhaps the cost and effort of the remodeling forces the store to raise prices higher than its competitors. Said store may even go out of business because it cannot compete if there is not enough income from the handicapped customers to pay for the changes. Somebody has to pay for the changes. Without the ADA, such changes are paid for directly by people who wish to benefit from that business for whatever reasons they choose.

The store that, on its own initiative, desired to implement change might very well get an income boost from patrons who appreciate that it went the extra mile for the individual who can use the store more easily. Perhaps community service awards and news coverage of the store's concerns will give that store far more publicity than the changes cost.

Whichever way such a two-store scenario turns out, I want you to understand that the first store is not hateful because it could not or would not make the changes. The owners based their decision to ignore the changes on business and social variables specific to them. Perhaps if they had spent the money to make the changes, their financial situation would not be able to bear the costs and the store would have to close, putting 100 employees out of work, decreasing the tax base, lowering the choice of goods for the residents who shop the area, and raising the prices by the loss of competition they could no longer provide.

Detractors of the free market argument ask where all the free market support was for the disabled before the ADA came along and forced such changes. The simple and correct answer is: all the disabled improvements that were needed were either in place or were underway.

The free market always takes care of its customers' needs. Always. I hope to present this more fully throughout future chapters. Even in a free market, however, places will exist where disabled folks cannot maneuver in certain businesses or organizations because the free market reacts to needs as quickly as it can—and no quicker. Such a government mandate boosts problems and solves very little. Once you learn about the ADA's costly changes and massive litigation in its first decade and a half, then see how its costs into future decades have no end in sight, you should agree that a lack of handicapped standards and accommodations in certain places was far less damaging to the handicapped than the damages incurred by the ADA.

In addition to increasing discrimination and resentment for the handicapped, ADA has caused other ill effects. Before the ADA was signed into law, major efforts were taking place in the free market to put into place handicapped parking areas. Malls and organizations built in the 1980s already had such parking places, and those were very good indeed because they were put there willingly and not by coercion. When an organization, on its own initiative, wants to install such facilities, the compassion is striking, touching, and appreciated by all.

When forced to park far from the door even though the ADA-required handicapped spaces up front all remain empty the day you need a space, a customer feels resentment. If the mall owners, knowing their customer base, could determine on their own how many disabled spaces were optimum then it would be rare to see an empty handicapped space when all of the non-disabled spaces were full. A customer's resentment is not as great if he or she knows that the mall put those spaces there by design and not because of a faceless, controlling law. The ADA's percentage and number rules for handicapped parking spaces ignore the needs of any specific community.

Or maybe without the ADA, you would feel just as much resentment of the company-installed handicapped spaces and you'd go to a different mall without them. Either response, resentment or no resentment, is legitimate and should not be legislated.

♿

DRIVING BLINDLY

Drive-up ATMs (Automatic Teller Machines), in the middle of nowhere, always seem to have Braille on their buttons. To be consistent, the ADA should also require that all cars have Braille steering wheels, speedometers, and temperature indicator gauges for any blind drivers who might be using those drive-up ATMs.

SHAKING DOWN THE PERMANENTLY DISABLED

After the ADA was signed into law, the state of Oklahoma (and probably most other states) designed at least two sets of handicapped parking permits: permanent ones and temporary ones that expired after a specific date. To get a permanent parking permit, you had to furnish a doctor's written notice that stated your disability was chronic and lifelong.

Someone having hip or knee surgery would be able to get the temporary permit for just as long as they needed but no longer. The two kinds of permits were distinctive; you could tell quickly which cars had the permanent permits and which had the temporary ones.

Less than a decade after issuing the permanent parking permits, Oklahoma decided to revoke all of the permanent handicapped parking permits and *only* the permanent ones. The unintended consequences of the ADA showed themselves once again to be alive and well. Police in at least one major Oklahoma city, Tulsa, were assigned to theaters, shopping malls, and other locales where many handicapped people might be found at one time. The police left tickets on every vehicle with a permanent parking permit. The ticket indicated that the permanent parking permit had expired and a fine was required. As Dave Barry would say, I am not making this up. Only the government would declare a permanent permit to be temporary years after it issued the permanent permit.

To add further insult to injury, the traffic division would not let those handicapped people with lifelong debilitating handicaps explain the situation by mail or phone. Every permanently-handicapped person issued the ticket had to go to Tulsa's City Hall, pay to park in the spaces provided, learning in the process that seemingly far fewer handicapped spaces are available at City Hall than required at most businesses, then go to an upper floor to the traffic violation division and demonstrate his or her disability. The traffic violation department would routinely take names and ticket numbers and tell the handicapped individuals to take a new permit request form to their doctors once again to sign. Then they had to mail that signed form and the ticket back into the traffic division, and then and only then would the ticket be expunged and a new, temporary permit be given. That is, as long as those permanently-handicapped people enclosed the required fee with their application.

Such bureaucratic red tape was a tremendous burden to every permanently-handicapped Tulsan—quite a few folks considering Tulsa's three quarters of a million people. A cynic has said that if Karl Marx were not agonizing in hell right now, he would be turning over in his grave wishing that he had thought of the ADA first.[12] You do not have to be a cynic to agree that these actions of the state government of Oklahoma are questionable at best.

The reason the state decided to revoke the permanent parking permits was because the state had lost control over who had permits. Some permits had been stolen (or sold to the highest bidder) and were being used by people who did not have the right to use them. Any forward-thinking American could have easily predicted this would happen; as so often is the case, the government had no idea that it would. And yet Tulsa did not need to require each and every vehicle owner using the permit to go through the aforementioned dance—and expense—to get replacements. A phone call or letter from the ticket holder was all that was needed to verify that the permit belonged to the person using it.

Oklahoma realized too many people were using the permits. Something had to be done about it. But as with so many countless instances, the government's response inflicted stress and expense upon the very people the law was designed to protect instead of just punishing those few who improperly used permits that didn't belong to them. The state of Oklahoma had absolutely no reluctance putting scores of truly handicapped people through this hoop-jumping process rather than taking responsibility to admit their own shortsightedness and cutting their losses. Yet, if any private business dares to cause a handicapped person one extra step in life, the full force of the government and its Department of Justice is there to patrol the situation, making sure that corrections are made and paid for by the business's checkbook and time.

MARKED OR MARRED?

That ubiquitous international handicapped symbol emblazoned upon permits, parking placards, signs, doors, ramps, bars, faucets, windows, and much more seems to carry an implied warning to any who dare disrespect its intentions.

Throughout history, people have had to wear certain symbols that showed they were different and had to be treated differently. The symbols served to separate those people from the normal population. As in parts of America before the 1960s, restrooms are now segregated to be used just by people who are different—those people known as "disabled persons." One wonders if the creators of ADA's statutes prefer to live, park, work, and even use bathrooms without getting close to, looking at, or, heaven forbid, actually having to help a handicapped man or woman themselves.

Disabled people now have their own entrances into many places that normal people are discouraged from using. How do the truly handicapped feel when, now, everywhere they go, they must bear the mark of the chair?

THE WORST IS AHEAD

Since the ADA was law, I have collected ADA-related articles, recorded insights, and stayed alert for its advantages and abuses. My personal interest grew out of a strong regret for not voicing my concerns about unexpected consequences before the ADA was passed. If there were ever a public issue that I regret not fighting to explain what I knew would be unexpected consequences, the Americans with Disabilities Act is that issue.

To its discredit, the ADA has far surpassed my expectations because I could not have guessed how much abuse would be instigated under its auspices. I knew it would be dangerous, but I had no clue that it would grow so rapidly, be exported to so many other countries so quickly, and be used by so many as a crutch. Those with crutches are people the ADA authors said they wanted to help; instead, the ADA itself became a crutch.

I did suspect that several distinct groups would adopt the Americans with Disabilities Act and use it as ammunition for their causes. I voiced this concern on national television at least once right after the ADA was signed into law. I did not, though, realize how far such groups would go to use the ADA for their own purposes, greed, and even criminal acts against society.

I wanted this first chapter to give you a broad sense of my position and to set the groundwork for why I suggest that the ADA fosters discrimination—exactly the opposite of its stated goals. I believe that a bad law cannot be fixed, it must be completely removed from the books before its ill effects will cease. I do not believe there is any hope of getting rid of the ADA; that time has long since passed, and the monster has escaped the cage. Too many people profit from the ADA's organizational structure both within and outside the government. I can only present this side of the ADA argument to give you some insight that you will likely not get elsewhere.

In the next chapter we will focus on numerous wily and cunning ways that shrewd people use the ADA for little more than personal gain or to further their social agendas to the detriment of many—including the handicapped.

2

ADA: "Abuses Do Abound"

*What else would you expect from a woman
who thinks her chocolate allergy entitles her to
park in a handicapped space?*
—Frasier Crane, *Frasier*

An indicator that a law is bad is the amount of abuse that occurs under that law's auspices. Even further evidence of bad law is when the people in charge of that law's jurisdiction enable, even promote, rampant abuse. This chapter exposes several instances of what some would consider being abuses of the Americans with Disabilities Act. Let me make it clear that some people, such as those initiating lawsuits like those mentioned here and those who work within the ADA's vast organizational command structure will disagree that these are ADA abuses; for them, they are simply justice duly meted.

Massive anecdotal evidence reveals a general trend. Such numerous case-by-case examples do suggest the existence of an underlying problem. By exposing these abuses of the ADA, I hope to show that the ADA is not only being used for ill but that the extent of that abuse indicates that this law should be rethought. I would never use anecdotal evidence alone to justify a law being good or bad. I want the conclusions I make in this book to be logical and result from a rational explanation of what is going on. Having said that, a raging pattern of abuse does require a strong review of whether a law is good or needs to be abolished completely.

Full Disclosure: I am not an attorney. I have had no formal training in law. Therefore, I have the ability to explain the ADA law's ramifications in clear, simple-to-understand language. Be warned that due to my lack of training as a lawyer, the ADA's consequences will make a great deal of sense to most who read *Disabling America*.

HE BET HIS DISABILITY

The San Jose, California, taxpayers came to the aid of a former police officer when the Police and Fire Retirement Board gave Johnny Venzon,

Jr., early retirement due to his disability.[1] Any community would rally to support a police or fire officer harmed in the line of duty. When one puts his life on the line for others, people are grateful. If a gunshot wound cripples an officer or a burning fire harms a firefighter, the wound is honorable and at the same time severely regrettable.

But what has concerned many about this situation is that Venzon and his counsel never claimed the disability due to an injury while on duty. Instead, this ex-cop was officially declared disabled due to his gambling addiction. Recall the previous chapter's argument against the term "disability" as opposed to the clearer term "handicap." You can see in this case why "handicap" is no longer welcome in the English language; even unscrupulous counsel (assuming any exist) would find it difficult to call a gambling addiction a handicap—unless we're talking horse races, of course.

This case just keeps on giving. That is, giving to Venzon. The Police and Fire Retirement Board awarded him $27,000 annually for his pension after granting the early retirement. The public coffers were tapped, and the spigot was opened wide. Medical experts surfaced who stated that the ex-cop's obsessive-compulsive gambling habit represented a pathological problem that effectively prevented him from being a police officer.[2]

To compound taxpayer frustration, this former officer was incarcerated for burglary at the time the board granted him his early retirement and $27,000-per-year pension. Venzon claims that he was forced to steal to support his gambling addiction. Could the burglary and incarceration have stood in the way of his retirement had the board not ruled that his newly-labeled disability caused him to commit burglary? Such a question is moot because the money was paid.

To say that a gambling "disability" forces one to steal is an offense to every truly-handicapped, law-abiding person in the world.

ADA AIDS AIDS

Carlo Morelli owned and managed *Raviolli's*, a small pasta parlor just north of Dallas in the early 1990s. He had retired from being a busy restaurant entrepreneur and wanted to run the small business in a way that imbued a community spirit. The pasta parlor quickly expanded from the restaurant to a community center, a banquet hall, and a catering operation that employed eighty-five people. The college town, Sherman, Texas, enjoyed the meeting place.

This was in the early days of the ADA. Morelli has told how he cheered the Americans with Disabilities Act when Congress debated the law.[3] Three of Morelli's family members are deaf. He said, "I thought anything we could do for disabled people would be good. If it inconvenienced us a little, it would probably be worth it."

But after five agonizing years and a personal financial loss of $300,000, Morelli quickly learned that the ADA's inconvenience far outweighed its benefit. He recounts, "The bureaucrats have turned this [ADA] into an ugly thing, divisive and mean, not what everyone envisioned it to be." He continues with great wisdom: "It's not an Americans with Disabilities Act. It's an Americans with Excuses Act."[4]

A kitchen worker, Jeremy, whom Morelli employed as a dishwasher, contracted AIDS. Sores began to break out on Jeremy's neck and arms. He had a nagging cough. Morelli expressed his concern for the employee with whom he says he got along well and whom he had no intention of firing. Word got out in the pasta parlor's small college town, and business started dropping. To make matters worse, Morelli says, "An AIDS patient has no immunities. That means Jeremy caught everything that was going around. When he caught a cold it darn near turned into pneumonia. TB [tuberculosis] is a problem, and I just couldn't have someone who came into contact with every utensil in the restaurant passing along communicable diseases. That's common sense."[5]

Morelli's dilemma was three-fold: he needed to protect Jeremy, to protect his other employees, and to protect his customers. Morelli asked Jeremy if he would be willing to move out of the kitchen where infections could spread and cause others trouble. Jeremy was offered a raise to do gardening and grounds work around *Raviolli's* and to run errands for Morelli. Jeremy left and returned with an Equal Employment

Opportunity Commission representative who told Morelli that Jeremy would stay in the kitchen.

Co-workers, out of an understandable fear of infection from an incurable communicable disease, began quitting. When word spread throughout the small community, the restaurant's receipts dropped from $129,000 to $32,000. When Morelli asked his lawyer what it would take to defend the restaurant against the EEOC's charges, one million dollars was announced as the cost. Seeing that the pockets of the ADA-empowered EEOC were far deeper than his own, Morelli closed *Raviolli's* after only eight months in operation.

HIDDEN ABUSE

The closing of *Raviolli's* made it unnecessary for the case to go to trial. Without a restaurant, discrimination against the disabled by the establishment could no longer be argued. Eighty employees lost their jobs, and many were forced to leave town. A community locale was closed. Jeremy neither got his raise nor was he able to keep working in the kitchen as it was no longer operating. Morelli lost $300,000 in legal fees and in costs he incurred by the closing. Customers lost food they enjoyed. The local real estate market lost in extra strain caused by the real estate that was now on the market.

The only one who had no loss was the EEOC officer. His status and job were never in danger—in fact, having gone to the mat for the disabled, his profile no doubt increased on the job.

How many situations have arisen since 1990 when President Bush signed the ADA legislation that, like *Raviolli's*, never get to court? The problem with these events is that the true number of businesses and employees and customers that have been harmed by these ADA-sponsored, over-compensating, cost-ignoring accommodations can never be counted because so many cases don't make it to the court system. Some would argue that keeping so many of these cases out of court is a plus to our bottlenecked judicial system. Such a justification is a false justification. The court system's docket was not burdened by Morelli's experience, but scores of other people were burdened. By not going to court where records are kept in detail, the scope, breath, and depth of the ADA's use and abuse will never fully be known.

In addition to the number of businesses that simply fold in the threat of an ADA attack, many settle before the cases get to court. If employers do fight the ADA charge, the American Bar Association has said that employers win more than 90 percent of the ADA court cases.[6] Although the American Bar Association might term these events as *wins*, the defendants could beg to differ.

Such a high percentage of wins should not be considered victories by any means. Christopher Bell was one of the architects of the Americans with Disabilities Act. He now represents businesses that need to defend against ADA cases, perhaps as a penance of sorts. Bell has said, "There absolutely is an element of intimidation. You say to an employer, 'Gee, you can settle this for $20,000, or we can litigate it and probably win but, if we win at the summary judgment level, it might cost, oh, $30,000, $50,000, $70,000; if we win after a jury trial it might cost $125,000.' Most businesspeople aren't going to like paying the $20,000 settlement, but it's a heck of a lot cheaper than the alternatives, and of course, plaintiffs' lawyers know that. So there is tremendous economic leverage for filing a lawsuit and getting some money."[7]

What do you suppose the chances are that headaches caused by trying to defend against ADA lawsuits are covered under the Americans with Disabilities Act?

FRIVOLOUS LEGAL COMPLAINTS

Dick Thornburgh, a former U.S. Attorney General, said in 2000 that 87 percent of the EEOC's ADA and related complaints have been found to be frivolous or were closed for "administrative reasons" instead of going all the way to court.[8] He sees this as a positive sign that attorneys will soon stop attempting such cases.

I don't follow the reasoning that an 87 percent frivolous case rate is a positive percentage, but then again I am not a lawyer so I have a more difficult time seeing good in this. What an incredible cost and burden on the EEOC to have listened to, researched, debated, and finally tossed out 87 percent of its cases. Just because these cases don't get to court doesn't mean they have zero cost. In fact, cases that don't get to court are often a huge strain on the defendants and whatever counsel is researching the case's justification. These massive costs could only be incurred by a governmental agency paid for by taxpayers; no private organization would have the unlimited funds needed to mess with an 87 percent frivolous caseload.

Thornburgh is also not considering the fact that from 1990 to 1991, 13,000 allegations of discrimination against the disabled were brought before the EEOC. A decade later, in 2000, the EEOC still admits that barely more than 10 percent of such cases are meritorious and worth pursuing. If such a high percentage of frivolous cases will cause a decline of filings, somebody apparently forgot to tell the American Bar Association and others who might be involved in filing these cases.[9]

THE ADA'S ROAR DEAFENS

Small, low-margin establishments such as *Raviolli's* and other restaurants seem to be breeding grounds for ADA cases. One busy restaurant was in need of a hostess to manage the hustle and bustle of tables as they were cleared. The hostess had to listen closely to guests' requests, guiding them to their tables, maneuvering around the wait staff as they carried plates full of food and drinks, keeping the new guests comfortable and moving while staying out of the way of bussing staff carrying stacks of trays and dishes yelling, "Excuse me!"

Completely able-bodied employees find such a job difficult. When a deaf woman applied enthusiastically, the owner realized that due to her deafness she could fail to hear a waitress coming with a hot pot of coffee or might not hear a tray full of food coming up behind when she's leading new guests through the diner. Having told her the risks, the owner started looking for another applicant. The deaf woman started looking for an EEOC lawyer.

Larry Elder, talk show host and author, has related this story in the past and concludes by explaining how he contacted the EEOC lawyer who represented this deaf claimant.[10] Elder asked the lawyer how he could justify action against this restaurant. Elder explained that the owner acted out of safety and common sense for the applicant, the other employees, and the customers. The lawyer responded that Congress created the ADA to get Americans to "think differently about the disabled." By not acting out of safety and common sense for all involved? Sadly, that goal is being achieved, case upon case, lawsuit upon lawsuit.

&

SAFETY TAKES A BACK SEAT TO BIG LAWSUITS

Consider how the coerced hiring of disabled workers in some high-risk positions can be irrefutably shown to put others at risk needlessly; the only conclusion you can draw is a financial reward for those on a lawsuit's plaintiff's side. James Bovard clearly sees the ADA advocates' seeming desire: "To find prized legal assets (the disabled) and create a powerful incentive to maximize the number of Americans who claim to be disabled."[11] You can easily understand why Bovard uses the phrase "Attorneys Dreams Answered" as the true meaning behind the letters ADA.

NOW, THE DEAF ARE BLIND

The National Football League often adheres to a blackout rule when a local stadium doesn't fill to sold-out capacity. If a game does not sell out at least seventy-two hours in advance of the kick-off, the game cannot be aired in its home venue. In other words, if seats are available at the game, the NFL doesn't want the game shown on local television because those seats are likely to remain unsold since the fans can stay at home and watch the game.

The wisdom of the blackout rule is perhaps arguable, but the NFL is the owner of its own broadcast, and if the NFL doesn't want a game showing somewhere on television then that is its right. At least, that seemed to be the case until attorneys for a Cleveland deaf group sued the National Football League over the blackout rule. By not showing the game on television the suit claimed that the NFL violated the rights of the hearing impaired.[12]

DEPENDENCE, INDEPENDENCE—
WHAT'S THE BIG DIFFERENCE?

So many ADA advocates want the workforce to provide independence for the disabled, no matter how much it costs and no matter how dependent the disabled employee must become on the employer. This facade of independence could be seen early when the ADA required that in some cases, "Businesses must hire people to work as readers, interpreters, or travel attendants to accommodate the needs of the disabled employees."[13]

James Bovard points out that soon after the ADA's signing, a large group of disabled advocacy groups showed outrage in July of 1991 that the ADA had not also required businesses to provide toilet assistants to the handicapped as a "reasonable accommodation" to achieve equal opportunity with other workers.

Taken to its extreme (comfortable territory for the ADA), consider a small kiosk-based business such as those found at malls across the country. This bathroom accommodation requirement would require two employees to be hired when normally only one non-disabled person might be able to handle the business. The second employee would be there to help whenever the disabled employee had to use the bathroom. Automatically, one-half of the population would be unable to fulfill this second position because only a second worker of the same sex would be able to enter the same bathroom to provide the help.

As a handicapped person, these kinds of stories offend my sense of dignity. A government bureaucracy, marshaled by the Department of Justice and ADA advocates, grows by leaps and bounds and invades all areas of American life. These people seek to decree that employers—

regardless of their needs or business interests—give me bathroom assistance. I may not need it and I may not take advantage of such service, but the fact that it's seriously considered as a part of the ADA umbrella gives me a creepy feeling that I can hardly shake without effort.

Why? In part, because it exposes the most obvious lie of the ADA: You cannot be independent and dependant at the same time.

The government's claim to bring independence to the handicapped is a fib. The ADA forces changes that actually result in handicapped people becoming more dependent—dependent on legally-coerced employers, government lawyers, and the entire ADA complex. This does more than just give a false sense of independence; regulations that force dependence by falsely promoting independence are disingenuous, deceitful, and devious.

WIDEN THE DOORS OR SHRINK THE WALLS

By declaring obesity to be a protected job disability, the Equal Employment Opportunity Commission adds to the disability roles, increases its importance, promotes further dependence, and in many ways convinces overweight people that they need to do nothing about their possible health dangers.

One man who weighed in at 410 pounds applied to the New York City Transit Authority for the job of subway train conductor. The Transit Authority passed on the applicant because he was too large to fit through the small cab doors on the train. He took the Transit Authority to court, and the courts agreed that the reasonable accommodation the Transit Authority should make was to widen every door of every conductor's train in the system.[14]

Many kinds of weight-based cases have been filed in the name of ending discrimination against the disabled. A Maryland teacher, Janice L. Pepperman, filed a lawsuit against the Gaithersburg school district claiming that she faced verbal taunts from other teachers. She said the taunts were based solely on her "genetic disorder." The disorder turns out to be that she is 5 feet 4 inches tall and weighs 230 pounds. At the time of the filing, Pepperman had taken sick leave due to poor health.[15]

Jennifer G. Hickey, in writing about this case, describes how under the EEOC's interpretation of the ADA, the term "impairment" cannot be applied to such general characteristics as hair, eye color, height, weight, or muscle tone. Therefore, just because an employee is over-weight does not provide grounds for a disability-discrimination claim. An employee who is morbidly obese or suffers from a psychological disorder that causes extreme fatness, however, does have a claim. Some of these weight-based cases are being dismissed by the federal courts while others are being taken. The drumbeat to squeeze the courts' resources marches onward.[16]

GETTING A GOOD SEAT

In another heavyweight lawsuit, a 360-pound Tennessee woman sued a movie theater chain for $1.5 million for emotional distress. She said that none of the theater seats was large enough to accommodate her. She was angry that the theater's management would not let her bring in and set up her own larger seat in the auditorium.[17]

If every seat were wide enough to accommodate that woman, would any seats be wide enough to accommodate the 410-pound Transit Authority applicant? Probably not. If every seat were wide enough to accommodate the 410-pound Transit Authority applicant, would the less gravity-challenged movie patrons be able to reach both arm rests?

This seat-width lawsuit is not the only way the ADA has tried to harass, even devastate, the movie theater industry. By the mid-1990s, the movie theater industry had come close to financial ruin. New theaters were being built, but customers were not coming in numbers large enough to pay for them. In addition, older theaters that contained only two or three screens could not find an audience. The industry got some relief when the stadium seating concept caught on. As the theater industry saw a chance to recover, the ADA, always sensing weakness, pounced.

AMC Entertainment, one of the leaders in providing stadium seating in most of their movie complexes, wants every moviegoer to enjoy their stadium seating so they provide several wheelchair spaces and special seating areas about one-fourth of the way up each auditorium's room. The areas are clearly marked and some seats are removed for the wheelchair bound. In addition, AMC provides hearing assistance devices for moviegoers who need them.

In 1999, Janet Reno's Justice Department brought suit against AMC Entertainment. The claim said the wheelchair-bound patrons were denied good seats and were cramped in the first few rows. United States District Court Judge Florence-Marie Cooper ruled that such movie theatres with stadium seating violate the Americans with Disabilities Act:

> A movie theater owner who provides wheelchair seating only in the front rows of the auditorium deprives persons with disabilities of equal access, benefits, and services in violation of the Americans with Disabilities Act.[18]

The ruling declared that AMC must provide wheelchair seating with comparable sightlines, which means all in wheelchairs need to be able to see from any row in the theater just as everybody else can.[19] How is AMC to provide wheelchair-bound seating on every row of the movie? Each aisle would have to be wide enough to accommodate wheelchairs, and that would cut down the number of rows in the auditoriums by at least a third. In addition, middle seats of each row would have to be removed so the wheelchairs had a place. Only then could a wheelchair-bound individual sit anywhere other moviegoers sit. But ironically, the middle-of-the-row wheelchair spaces would prevent the other moviegoers from these middle seats. By demanding equality, the ADA creates inequality.

Non-ADA movie discrimination suits can now appear due to this ruling. If AMC's handicapped patrons are discriminated against because they don't get to sit in the upper-third of the theater, then anybody who buys a ticket to the movie late and can only find a seat in the lower-third is discriminated against. They are not given the full stadium-seating experience any more than their handicapped peers who must suffer down front with them.

Chris Stamper writes about this ruling and correctly imagines the costly nightmare for AMC and other owners who now face major renovations in thousands of auditoriums across the United States.[20] The upper stadium seats of many auditoriums can only be reached by stairs, necessitating some kind of elevator system being squeezed into each auditorium in addition to aisles being widened and seats being removed in the upper rows.

This ruinous lawsuit hits home with your author. As you learn more about my life, you will see how and why the full exposure of the Americans with Disabilities Act is important to me. One problem is that I was born with one leg. As much as I would like to hide that fact from the ADA government workers who want to control my life, I'm disclosing the fact rather openly here.

The reason that this lawsuit against the AMC movie theatres strikes home is that this poor, crippled-up, one-legged *Disabling America* author enjoys the AMC stadium seating experience. In fact, I have seen more movies at the Tulsa AMC theater than anybody else in the entire state. I was the first to reach their former VIP level of 15,000 points in their *AMC MovieWatcher* club. Due to the enormous number of movies I have seen there, I know most of the employees, and they know me.

I never could have seen so many movies at that AMC theater if an ADA official had thought to tell me first that my disability keeps me from viewing movies.

SAFETY LAST

While an enjoyable night to the movies suffers (along with the entire theater industry), so does safety. Consider the case of a local YMCA chapter sued for $20 million by a "profoundly" deaf lifeguard. The YMCA assumed that lifeguards should be able to hear yells and distress signals. When, however, they sought to replace the deaf lifeguard with one who could hear cries for help, the lifeguard sought counsel.[21]

The inclusion of the elderly in the Americans with Disabilities Act's fluid definition of "disabled" has forced many states and municipalities to change their hiring requirements for police officers. They have been forced to put into place sliding-scale fitness tests to accommodate older and female applicants.[22] (At the time of this writing, I could find no complaints about this ADA suggestion that all females are disabled.)

In 1995, a Coloradoan sheriff's deputy, David Bell, was fired because he did not meet the Jefferson County "fitness-for-duty" standards. Bell contacted the Equal Employment Opportunity Commission and filed a complaint under the ADA's statutes. Surprisingly, the suit was tossed out, but two years later Bell sued the county again. The county settled out of court for $110,000 instead of taking the case to trial.[23]

Consider the Exxon Valdez oil-spill disaster in Alaska in 1989, allegedly caused by the tanker's inebriated captain. Exxon later ruled that employees with histories of drug or alcohol abuse couldn't hold safety-sensitive jobs. But the EEOC doesn't see why drug and alcohol abuse should keep one from holding a safety-related position. Amazingly—in complete disregard for the safety of even the drug– or alcohol-abusing employee, let alone everyone else—the EEOC says such a position is discriminatory under the Americans with Disabilities Act.[24]

Bad ideas often have deadly consequences. If one person dies after someone is hired without any regard to that person's possible safety risk to others, the guilt falls equally on the hands of everybody who supported such absurdity. Consider the lack of wisdom shown if one hires a deaf lifeguard and someone drowns or if an unqualified police office fails to stop a crime that a more able-bodied officer could very well have prevented in time. When a government regulatory committee creates a law implemented by organizations such as the EEOC and ADA advocates without any accountability, any and all such guilt will never be admitted or identified.

NOT JUST A CAN OF WORMS BUT A SNAKE PIT

Is the inability to be without snakes a disability? In one case, mentioned by a guest on National Public Radio's *Diane Rehm Show*, which was hosting a celebration of the ADA's ten-year anniversary, an employee claimed a phobia of *not* being around snakes.[25]

Citing the ADA's protection, he requested that his employer allow him to bring his pet snake to work. I was surprised that in spite of the fact that the show aired on NPR, where absurdity is often complimented, the guest did admit that this particular claim was far-fetched. I almost beg to differ. Given the abuses that have been approved in the ADA's short history, can you blame the snake lover for making such an attempt? Fortunately it appears the snake suit was tossed out before being heard.

RARE OCCURRENCE:
THE TRULY DISABLED TRIUMPHS

Much common sense in American society has been eliminated on the altar of the ADA and political correctness, the ADA's preferred mode of transportation. So many new ways of regulating American life have arisen that, once in a while, one politically-correct idea is pitted against another. The ADA is now beginning to show up as one of the parties in these contests.

For instance, how will the sexual harassment regulations be honed over time so as not to include persons with sexual dysfunctions now considered to be disabilities? When a sexual harassment defendant goes up against a deviant who claims his deviancy is a disability, the sexual harassment pundits are then pitted directly against the ADA pundits, and their causes oppose one another in court. In many such cases, both sides' attorneys win fame, peer respect, and legal fees; everybody else just loses.

Having said that, once in a while when two politically-correct forces clash, purely by chance, justice actually gets served. Sometimes the truly harmed come out victorious in the courts. Such a case occurred in Maryland after a father, at his own expense, built a thousand-foot brick pathway so that his daughter Leah could enjoy a nearby tributary named Glebe Creek. He built the pathway because Leah has muscular dystrophy and uses a wheelchair.

The father did not request ADA-related funds to build the pathway. The father did not ask for the highway department to install the pathway. The father did not ask for special tax provisions for the pathway. Most important, the father built the pathway on private property.

The fact that the pathway was on private property did not deter the county code-enforcer who said the pathway violated the state's Critical Area Act, which mandates a hundred-foot, no-building zone around designated bodies of water.[26] The state's Critical Area Commission took the case before a county circuit judge who agreed that the pathway had to be removed.

The father took his case to the Maryland Court of Appeals soon afterwards. That court said the path could stay. The reason given was that the ADA grants public agencies wide latitude in accommodating people with disabilities.

If only the ADA granted private agencies and business any latitude.

&

THE SHORTEST ROUTE

All the huge theme parks, such as Six Flags and Universal Studios, and public venues such as Atlantic City's Boardwalk parking lots have the required handicapped parking spaces right next to the entrance gates. Suppose one of those parks consume 8 square miles of real estate; by parking in the handicapped spaces up front, these disabled persons now only need to traverse a more manageable 7.9 miles. Good intentions have once again tossed out common sense with the full force of the Department of Justice behind them.

PROMISES TO BREAK

On June 27, 2000, The National Council on Disability released a 380-page report named *Promises to Keep*. The report harshly criticized federal agencies for their poor track record in enforcing the Americans with Disabilities Act. NCD chairperson Marca Bristo said agencies had been "overly cautious" in enforcing the law and that "poor leadership" has significantly weakened the law's impact.[27]

How much more would have been done if these agencies were not overly cautious? I cringe after reading through some of the lawsuits brought forth under the guise of the ADA and think of what may have resulted if those who police the ADA had better, more ambitious leadership.

A FLUID LAW

Not only has the ADA's own definition and determination of the meaning of "disabled" changed, the law itself has changed. Recently lawmakers have begun to look at the ADA and its consequences in a new light. After more than a decade of what some would call extortion-like litigation, the Supreme Court and lawmakers have made some provisions that promise to hone the ADA somewhat. One can only hope that such measures will begin to stop the forward momentum this law has gained. Abuses such as those cited in this chapter are just a drop in an ocean of costly, hamstringing regulations.

3

Confessions of a Handicapped Man

She asked me, "Do you blame your mother?"

The woman had just sat down next to me. I looked at her for the first time in my life and queried, "Excuse me, what did you ask?"

I was attending a California wedding and knew nobody in this huge reception hall except for my wife Jayne and the bride.

She continued, "I asked if you blamed your mother . . . for your disabilities?"

I said, "You must work either in the psychiatric or legal profession to ask a complete stranger such an insulting question."

She said that she was a psychologist. I quietly but promptly moved to a different table.

I often stop to remind myself how grateful I am. I was born, educated, and entered adulthood in a pre-ADA world.

I can hardly imagine how different life would be if I had been born after 1990. That is, assuming I *was* born. I cannot take for granted that a doctor or some state-funded social caregiver assigned to my mother would not have tried to convince her that I could not fully enjoy my life with only one leg and a grand total of three stubby fingers.

I invite you into my own life for the next few pages. I ask that you let me describe being handicapped in America past and present. If I had been born without handicaps there is no way I could write this book for you. How else would someone be able to view the Americans with Disabilities Act honestly and with passion? I'm not saying that one must be handicapped to understand, approve, or disapprove of the ADA. I'm not saying that one cannot understand if he or she hasn't walked the proverbial "mile" in my shoes. What I do hope to clarify is that the ADA always resounds loudly with me because of my handicaps whereas it obviously does not fully impact many others who have no such problems.

Many handicapped people have been born since 1990, the ADA's genesis year. Some of them will thrive in life. Some of them will do okay. Some of them will not do well. In other words, their successes will mirror the lives of those without handicaps. Having said that, why does the American government work to hamstring these folks further with the ADA? I think my life would have been much worse, perhaps horrible, if they had passed the ADA before my birth.

FORTUNATELY, MY WORLD CAME BEFORE

Because of when I was born, I'll never know if I could have overcome my handicaps with all the added obstacles the ADA puts in front of people like me. Such factors would have impacted me negatively but to what extent I'll never know. Programs I could have been assigned to would attempt to teach me how to walk, how to write, and when to take prescribed medicines and routine counseling—for only with their medications and counseling could I possibly cope with my disabilities. Such nonsense would have been detrimental to my future. I need no crystal ball to know that because I know myself well.

I do imagine a worst-case scenario. Chances are much more probable that I would have turned out somewhere between my current life and my imagined worst-case scenario, but I'll tell you that worst-case scenario in a few moments. It's startling.

This is the kind of book that becomes personal between readers and the writer. The book's opponents will take a different personal view from those who read it and grasp my contention that the Americans with Disabilities Act and regulations and laws related to it harm the very people it purports to help. Many people feel differently. But in these controversial pages, I'm opening my life to you and giving you an insider's look at how the handicapped face life. Fortunately, I can almost count the number of people on one hand who have been as rude to me as the woman described in this chapter's opening. And considering *my* hands, that number is very low.

SUCCESS IS RELATIVE

In July of 1961, I was born the only child of Glen and Bettye Perry. They are still my happily-married parents. By itself, that makes my life a success. I didn't cause their marriage success but rather it was they who caused my success in life. And I'd do without any other success, whatever "success" happens to mean, as long as I still have them as parents.

I was born with a total of three fingers and one leg. My fingers are short, only one of which has a partially mobile joint. My right leg ends at my knee and cones down dramatically thereafter.

The origin of my problems is unknown. I was not a "thalidomide baby."[1] Thalidomide was a drug that appeared in 1957 to help West German pregnant women overcome morning sickness. Its use spread for only a few years because a direct link was discovered between thalidomide and physical deformities. These days, it's only doctors who ask me if I was a thalidomide baby, perhaps because it's been so long out of the mainstream of consciousnesses. Good riddance.

There was no apparent outbreak of other handicapped infants around that time. Both my parents were healthy when I was born. Thanks to healthy parents, I was a healthy child. They say the nurses called me "fatty." I'm still working on that problem.

My infancy was normal. I crawled when ready to do so. I got my first artificial leg when it was time to walk. So I walked. It was time.

I began picking up writing instruments a few months later. I used both hands to hold crayons, pens, and pencils. A well-meaning orthopedic doctor told my parents that he could operate on my right hand so that the two fingers there would close to grasp a pencil. This would give me an opposing grasp in that one hand. He performed the operation. As soon as I recovered, I picked up my crayon with both hands and began drawing again. I still use both hands today to write. I simply cannot fathom what is wrong with the two-handed method I use to write. I obviously didn't see why I should change back when I was two years old either.

When I went to school, they graded elementary students in penmanship. I don't know if they still do today. (If not, they should.) I got A's, B's, and C's for penmanship throughout my schooling. I distinctly remember that if I wrote well, I'd get A's, and if I got sloppy, I'd get C's—just like all the other kids who found out their penmanship grade reflected how hard they'd tried to avoid sloppiness. I never considered that my hands' physical layout had anything to do with my penmanship because it didn't. When I try to do something well, I do it better than when I'm sloppy. Just like everybody else.

MY MOM'S CONTRIBUTION

My mother was a teacher. So she did what teachers used to do, and that was teach me to read and write. When I got to kindergarten it was obvious to all that I was abnormal—I could read—so that year was often spent on my teacher's lap, in front of the class, reading books to my classmates during story time.

Mainstreaming was not an experiment that would hit the public schools for twenty-five or more years, so my reading skills were encouraged in school. When I entered the first grade, I would leave my regular class to attend an advanced three-student reading seminar for an hour or so daily. The reading was challenging, though I didn't like the fact that the other two students were girls.

I was promoted from the first grade to the third grade along with one of those other readers. One of the *girls*. My father kidded me that I skipped the second grade because the second-grade teachers didn't want me. He would be policed into counseling today for saying that. Back then, I thought it was as funny as he did so I repeated the joke for years when someone asked why I skipped the second grade. From my experience, I can relate the only problem with skipping the second grade: you will be the only high school freshman who cannot yet drive. That's a difficult one to hide.

My mother's contribution to my mental and emotional capabilities made everything else in life possible for me. Today, self-esteem is taught as a priority in schools and counseling sessions, but that seems so backwards to me. Being able to read, at four years old, the road signs your family drives by instills a lifetime of self-esteem.

MY DAD'S CONTRIBUTION

When I was about three years old, my father brought home a baseball, a baseball glove, a bat, and a football. That's what fathers do when their sons turn three. Sons then pick up the baseball, glove, bat, and football (not all at the same time) and begin playing. So that's what I did.

Dad took me to all the local minor-league baseball games. We went to college football games. We spent a lot of time together. Unfortunately for the both of us, my mother was hospitalized with tuberculosis for nine months when I was around three. Every Sunday, his only full day off from selling tires so we could eat and pay the mortgage, Dad would drive me one-hundred-plus miles so we could spend the day where my mother was hospitalized. It takes a real man to do that while raising his boy. It takes a real woman to hold up to the strain of being away from her husband and young son. Neither of my parents knows that, as an adult, I have several times come to tears thinking of what toll that must have taken on them.

The nights were for Dad and me. He took me to any and all games in town—baseball, football, hockey—we didn't care what it was, we loved it. I knew all the players on the Tulsa Oiler baseball team. They'd invite me into their dugouts and onto the field before each game. Naturally, Dad got me my own Tulsa Oiler baseball uniform to wear because no self-respecting three-year old would have shown up to a game without one.

With all of this going on, I couldn't wait to play ball. One day Dad took me outside, gave me the bat, and tossed a baseball to me. So I hit the ball. I recall running around imaginary bases sometimes after hitting the ball. I was always a fast runner. Dad then handed me the baseball glove and walked away—so I put it on. He tossed me the baseball. So, I caught it. Some time later, it was football season. Dad threw a football pass to me. So I caught it. Took me awhile to catch a pass while running because that takes some practiced coordination. I practiced, got some coordination, and then I could do it. My dad thought I'd be a good football kicker. He was wrong: I couldn't kick worth anything and still can't today, though I did become an incredible punter.

What is vital for you to understand is that my father did not start out trying to figure a way for me to hold the bat. He just gave me the bat. If he had first attempted to rig some kind of strap to it, I doubt I could have ever used a bat. My father did not get a leather-smith to make me a special baseball glove. He just got a regular glove at the store, and I put it on and used it every time I played.

My father is smarter than everybody behind the ADA who assumes every handicapped child, adult, and senior citizen need help. Those regulators force the world to adapt instead of waiting for the disabled to determine, and then seek, what they actually need.

If I had not been able to throw a baseball, catch a baseball, hit a baseball, catch a football, or punt a football, then that would have been okay, too. Dad did not expect me to be able to do all those things because not every boy can do all those things. I just happened to be a boy who could. Had I required any kind of contraption to make one or more of those things work for me, Dad would have been the first to get it made for me.

I never threw a football when I was younger. I'm not sure why. Dad would toss it, I would catch it, then I'd punt it back to him. I plainly remember realizing one afternoon, years later, when I was twelve years old and still a football fanatic, that I'd never attempted to throw a football pass. Throwing a football requires much different work than throwing a baseball. You must grasp the larger-than-your-hand pigskin in such a way that, with the laces facing up, your wrist can snap the ball at the last second to spin the ball into a perfect spiral. Otherwise, the ball flies end-over-end and never hits its target. Could I throw that perfect spiral pass? If not, I had enough to keep me busy. It turned out that I could.

BOTH PARENTS' CONTRIBUTION

As you can see, the primary contribution my parents made, the most important contribution to my life, was that they treated me like a son. They didn't treat me like a handicapped son. But I had handicaps. Both they and I had to deal with my hands and leg. I'd often come home from running or playing ball with skin blistering inside my artificial leg. That pain was horrible. I have a higher tolerance for pain as an adult because of all the pain I had with my leg as a child.

I happened to be able to do all the ball-related activities I wanted to do to keep myself happy. But I was not exceptional at any of these activities (though I was a better punter than anybody else my age for years), I was just average. But life brought many things that I could not do. Two weeks at a summer camp, for example, never entered our minds. I don't sleep with my artificial leg on and getting to the showers and bathrooms simply didn't make summer camp alluring to me.

Someone gave me a guitar when I was about six. I couldn't play it! How could I manipulate chords with one finger while strumming with my other hand? I put the guitar aside after about eight minutes and went on to something else. I really wanted to be able to shoot a bow and arrow when I was a kid. It seemed everybody had one of those rubber-tipped arrow sets. I really never found a good way to do it. I couldn't because I had three fingers. Yes, my handicap kept me from being able to do these things I wanted to do. But the handicap didn't depress me and neither did finding things I couldn't do.

Fortunately, as an adult I no longer want to shoot bows and arrows. I'm a great marksman, and my pistol, semi-automatic handgun, rifle, and shotguns fill that void when I participate in my now-favorite activities of target practice and skeet shooting.

I find things all the time I can and cannot do. That's life. My parents' attitude was: Here's a guitar, if you need help we'll get it, if not then have fun, and if you just can't do it, there are plenty of other things in life. I would guess that nineteen out of twenty people I know with a full set of fingers cannot play the guitar. Yet in my nightmares, I can envision ADA officials trying to think of ways to eliminate guitar sales because of how they harm the self-esteem of those who haven't the finger set needed to play a B7 chord.

FORMATIVE YEARS WERE DANGEROUS

Then the whirlwind began. What transpired between my hitting that first baseball and today will give you my idea of how the Americans with Disabilities Act could have ruined everything for me. Only when you see what you have, do you begin to imagine how many things could be taken away by different circumstances and approaches to life.

Throughout grades three through twelve, I was an average student. My academic excellence began and ended with the skipping of the second grade. Fortunately, I loved playing the trombone and so my marching band, jazz band, and orchestra grades helped offset some of my lower grades, and I ended up with average grades upon graduation.

My parents' struggle to save enough to buy me a Hammond organ that I wanted so very much when I was about eight gave me the ability to appreciate musical instruments. I'd joke that because of my hands I had to play by ear. Playing the organ actually led to my trombone playing. About the time I started those organ lessons, kids stopped playing the organ in general. I would play my Hammond organ for Tulsa's largest bank, The First National Bank, each Christmas season in their lobby when I was in high school. All the newspapers, radio and TV newscasts thought that was a big deal for me to do, and it was fun, but around my peers I never stressed my keyboard ability too much. It just wasn't hip. So I played the trombone.

About those average grades: I maintained just enough of an average to get by, with lots of help from my band-related classes, because I was lazy! I am unsure what happened during those years other than the continued degradation in public education, but I did enough to get by and no more. Let me bring you back to the Americans with Disabilities Act here and tell you why I think my teen laziness is critical to this book's discussion: If absolutely anybody had offered me special courses, special assistance, special accommodations, any excuse whatsoever that might have taken away my own responsibility from having to study or do any mundane task related to learning, I would have *jumped* at the chance!

I do *not* imply that most handicapped people who utilize aspects of the ADA today are not self-reliant, and I want to stress that. But I experienced years, very formative years, where I would have been completely harmed by such offers. As it was, without that kind of "help," I was basically a teenager who got by. I was one of those "good kids" because I never really did anything really bad (too often), but I never did anything really good either. I could have gone either way, and just a nudge from the ADA counselors could easily have pushed me into an attitude of entitlement for the rest of my life in spite of the solid foundation my parents gave me.

Here's proof of this. When my tenth grade math class got to geometry and it was time for the test, my teacher took me aside and said that she knew I couldn't handle a compass, ruler, and protractor so during the test I was to go to another teacher's planning period and she would take the test for me. I would tell her what to do, and she would draw the answers as I described, using the geometric tools that had been taught. My immediate thought was this: Wow, if I don't know an answer or if I show uncertainty on any part of this thing, she'll surely give me a hint. She did. I got a far better grade than if I had not had my helper.

What neither of those teachers knew was that I had been drawing my Marvel comic book heroes for years. To draw the background buildings and water tanks and cities, I had been using the compass, protractor, and rulers I had at home near my drawing tablets. I figured what they didn't know would only help me. But in reality it didn't help me at all. If they had first asked if I could handle the test on my own, I would have said yes. They assumed, however, that I couldn't. This was long before the school system began getting the real big bucks for labeling students "disabled," so such situations are far more numerous today.

GREAT EXPECTATIONS

I knew my parents wanted me to go to college, but that meant studying, and I didn't want to start *that*. Even so, I was a voracious reader. From an early age, I studied fields such as electronics, classic books, comic books, self-help (it was the 1970s), vitamins and natural health care (before it was cool), and many subjects nobody else my age knew or cared about. I read at least one book during each school day as long as it had nothing to do with the class subject. I finally resolved how to attend college, not have to study, fool my parents, have fun, and still get a degree. I'd major in psychology!

I applied for college a hundred miles away because I wasn't too keen on my parents knowing how little I planned to work at school. The small, struggling university welcomed my mediocre high school performance, and I enrolled as a first-year psych major. I knew I could ace any class in psychology without effort because during junior high and high school I'd read maybe a hundred psychology and counseling books and I knew how simple that subject would be. My plan was in place. After four years, I could coast through life being a psychologist which would give me plenty of time to read what I wanted, play the trombone, and still get paid without having to maintain a real skill set.

A funny thing happened on the way to my freshman year.

The summer before I planned to train for my career in psychology (*wink*), a friend who managed a local Radio Shack asked if I wanted want to work as a stock clerk during the week and a sales clerk on weekends. I loved electronics, stereos, CB radios (my handle was *Blue Jeans*), and scanners. I devoured each new Radio Shack catalog that arrived and spent hours in Radio Shack when I went to the mall. I thought: Get paid for doing what I would have paid them for? Where do I sign? Take me now, God, my life is complete!

By the way, nowhere on my employment paperwork did a check box appear asking if I had a disability. Those were the good old days. Just last week, I filled out a doctor's office form. It had next to "Sex" three choices: Male, Female, and Other. A classic joke has become a sad reality in my lifetime. It's like we're living in a *Seinfeld* episode, except this one isn't funny.

I loved that first week at Radio Shack stocking, putting those precious batteries and cables and eight-track players on the shelves. On my first Saturday, I was supposed to wear a tie because I would be handling the small spillover sales so the full-time sales staff could handle the larger merchandise. This was a very busy store on weekends. Ironically, it turned out that I knew far more about those products than the full-time sales staff. Customers asked me questions, and I knew the answers. Customers asked other salespersons questions, and I would have to answer those too. At the end of the day, the sales were tallied. I was the top salesperson for the day. I would not turn seventeen for a month, but

I was a success at something, and the ADA had absolutely nothing to do with it.

Ken, my manager, immediately told me to show up for work in a tie every day that I wanted to work. The second month I worked, July, I had the highest sales in the Tulsa region, and that included about twenty-five stores. I may have accidentally grabbed that confidential sales report where I was listed as number one the moment my manager filed it away because I still have it in my scrapbook. Ken, if you're reading this, I ask your forgiveness.

In August, Ken told me that nobody in Radio Shack knew anything about something called the company's first "microcomputer." He said that the headquarters simply had no training in place yet to teach the sales staff. Neither Ken nor anybody else in the store knew how to turn it on. He told me, "If you want to sell one of those things you should open the manual and learn what it says." I loved electronics, but I didn't have a desire to learn computers. I did enjoy my July commission check though, so I figured I could learn enough to be the first to sell a computer in the store.

I stayed late and opened the computer manual to page one. A new love entered my life. I sold three computers in August.

With my August Radio Shack commission check, I bought one of those microcomputers to take with me to college. As soon as I arrived, I scoured the technical libraries for any and all books about computers. They were advanced, difficult to understand, and written by computer programmers who programmed well and wrote badly. I took every single computer course offered by that university (a grand total of four) my freshman year. I realized that I'd do better at computers if I knew something about math. (I had previously learned that you don't have to know math to pass the subject in high school.) I signed up for introductory math courses each of those two semesters and loved math for the first time in my life. I increased my self-instruction on the computer to cover areas the college simply was not advanced enough to teach. This was 1978. The odds are great that I was the first college freshman in the world who spent more time at his own computer than at college parties.

I earned straight A's my second semester. My course load was heavy on the math and pre-user-friendly computer subjects, but for the first time in my life I had a passion that was consistent with a career path. I made plans to move home and attend the University of Tulsa the following year where they had a more advanced computer science curriculum. Because I didn't change my psych major my freshman year, I had to complete the courses I had enrolled in. But I didn't want to waste time, either. I made sure to attend psychology classes only on exam days. And, yes, I aced them.

My life flew when I began my real college courses in my real major of computer science, which they called "Information Systems." The first national magazine for the Radio Shack computer appeared on the stands. I never learned how to write well in school, but I knew that computer. I wrote an article and mailed it to the magazine. They sent me a check a week later and published my article in the next issue. I wrote another article, and they sent another check. I thought, "This is quite a racket!" I kept doing it. I liked the money, and I liked seeing my articles in the store magazine racks. I had no idea at the time where *that* would lead me.

Some have told me my adult life should be published as an autobiography. I disagree. It was my childhood journey that was important. My adult accomplishments just reflect what went before.

To see what a pre-ADA world enabled me to do, perhaps it's important to see my career path from college to the present. I hope parents of handicapped children who read this can take extra hope at this path of mine.

I graduated from the University of Tulsa with a 3.7 GPA and a computer science degree.

I was president of Kappa Sigma, a college fraternity. I was president of Omicron Delta Kappa Honor Society and treasurer of Mortar Board Honor Society. In my senior year, the college alumni voted me one of the college's "Ten Outstanding Seniors." I then received the highest award possible, the University of Tulsa's "Man of the Year."

I went straight into the college's MBA program and received my master's degree with an emphasis in corporate finance.

In 1986, I went to work for a Fortune 500 company, and in three years I was the youngest supervisor in the company's huge headquarters. A new world was dawning because the hiring clerk asked me why I didn't mark that I was disabled on my employment papers. I had seen that box, but it never entered my mind to check it. At first I thought she was confused, and then I realized what she was talking about. I told her that I didn't consider myself disabled. I then asked her if the company got special tax benefits if they had more workers who were disabled. She said yes. I let her mark it. I would never in my life allow that today. I would gladly lose the job than take that mark. ADA proponents will say I'm in denial. I'll say I'm not disabled. I'll then challenge them to a rollerblade race, and we'll see who's in denial.

Computers were growing in popularity, and books on computers began appearing in bookstores. But they were still badly written. I sent a letter to a publisher of these books. I was unsure of the protocol, so I just told them in a three-sentence letter that I liked computers, I had written many articles about computers, and that I'd be an excellent author for one of their books. Within two days, an Osborne/McGraw-Hill acquisitions editor called me. One week later, I signed a contract for my first book. I was twenty-five.

After five years, the corporate life was getting in the way of my writing, so I began teaching computers full time at a local college while still writing books about computers.

But by 1994, the teaching life was getting in the way of my writing, so I officially declared myself a full-time author and left the college arena.

In 1997, I was named one of the Ten Outstanding Young Tulsans by the Council Oak Junior Chamber of Commerce (the Tulsa Jaycees organization).

Growing up, I was churched but never saved which is somewhat like going to public school but never getting an education. One night I accepted Jesus Christ as my personal Savior. What a waste my life would have been without Him: full success on earth, overcoming perceived odds, all to disappear and be counted as loss in the end. (When the children of fellow Christians ask me why my hands are the way they are, their parents tell them "That's the way God made him." I gently correct those adults and say, "Actually, it's due to man's sin that these kinds of problems exist, but someday I'll have a new body." (That's a promise that no governmental regulation can provide, especially those that offer people false salvation like the ADA.)

I helped produce and guest host a nationally-syndicated television talk show for a few years.[2] I didn't accept payment because it was fun. I always tried to bring up the ADA on every show. I figured that a national broadcast platform was a good place to start talking about this important issue.

My father enjoys being a landlord with several rental properties, so I decided to I acquire and fix up several myself. I had a tremendous amount of help from him, but even with that help I couldn't see why people hated being landlords. I made a living helping people who hate computers like them, so I decided to write a book that showed reluctant landlords how to enjoy their job. That book has seen three editions and has been continually in print for a decade.[3]

I was the first author to reach the two-million-books-sold mark at one of my publishers, the largest computer book publisher in the world, Pearson Education. They publish my books under the publishing imprints of Sams Publishing and Que Publishing.

Along the way I met and married Jayne. Very special Jayne. The ultimate wife and still my bride. Knowing and loving her has made me a better man. She also helped to solidify my understanding of this book's issues. Jayne has traveled the world with me. For each of ten years, we spent approximately two months out of the country somewhere north, south, east, or west, looking at places we'd only dreamed of. From the icy waters surrounding Tierra Del Fuego, to hiking atop New Zealand's ice glaciers, to exploring the hot sands around Egypt's pyramids, we've enjoyed and learned about God's creation. Being an author has its advantages for me and for you. The advantage for *you* will be seen when you read a later chapter entitled "The ADA around the World." We always find our way back to Italy which is our first love as travelers. A new home has kept us busy for the past three or four years, but we can't wait to return to *bell' Italia* where we've mastered the language fundamentals and now stay with our dear, across-ocean friends from Venice to Rome to Sicily who know no English. The saddest part of traveling has to be the scores of new international disabled signs that we see popping up via new government regulations in every country.

♿

DRIVING BLINDLY

When touring the Valley Forge National Historical Park a few years ago, Jayne and I noticed a reserved handicapped parking space that we'd never seen before or since. This sign was the parking space closest to the gift shop's front door. Immediately below the expected wheelchair symbol, the sign displayed bold uppercase lettering that read, GOVERNMENT EMPLOYEES ONLY.

I have not yet been able to determine if the wheelchair symbol on top of the sign trumps the Government Employees Only text. Can a non-governmental handicapped guest use the space as the ADA intended it to be used? Or, are government employees the only ones allowed to park there even if they are not handicapped? Finally, one could wonder if government employees in wheelchairs are the only ones who can park there legally. (A friend once suggested that the sign implies government employees are all disabled, but I would never make such a claim.)

With more than seventy-five books under my belt and more on the way, each published internationally and translated into every major language, I've been told that I have written more computer books than anybody on earth.

And it was all because Mom taught me to read and Dad handed me a baseball bat when I was three years old.

HOW IT COULD HAVE BEEN

What could be different with the ADA in my life? Thinking about the detrimental effects of growing up and being schooled in an ADA world depresses me. Therefore, I'll keep it short because what little I say will ruffle enough feathers in the ADA camp.

I think I would have been a loser. I wouldn't be married. I'd be taking all the disability payments they'd dole out to me. How can I say this while at the same time crediting my parents previously with creating such a foundation? It's because I know myself. During my formative years throughout school, I would have happily taken any and every excuse to ditch all responsibility in my life—and I didn't have many responsibilities to ditch. If someone had told me that I could, because I am disabled, get paid just for being disabled, I assure you that I would have stopped being able to do all sorts of things.

I am not implying that everyone who accepts disability-related services and payments is shirking responsibilities. I am speaking for myself. I know myself. But I also know human nature, and if you think other handicapped individuals are not similarly inclined, you're missing something.

People tell me that it's remarkable what I've done in my life. They mean well, but they give me far too much credit. I simply see success as easier than failure—it's easier to sleep at night as a productive citizen with the bills paid. Even easier though would be to be handed everything. Being a victim requires doing absolutely nothing.

Government-legislated wheelchair ramps, wide doors, and bathroom grab bars mean that many handicapped people get along better due to changes imposed by the ADA. But it is the cost everyone pays that makes this deal a lemon. ADA-generated discrimination of the handicapped harms them in ways they may never see. Arguing that the ADA benefits many is not just insipid, it is specious.

I do not blame those who milk the Americans with Disabilities Act and all its related perks, lawsuit wins, out-of-court settlements, and the lower societal expectations that come with being an ADA victim. I blame the people who created the ADA and who administer it today.

The real ADA victims are the truly handicapped and the general public who pay the bill.

A NOTE TO NEW PARENTS
OF A HANDICAPPED CHILD

I did not know that I was handicapped for many years. I recall someone first telling me that I was handicapped when I was six or seven. By then I was past any tendency to worry about it. Then, the world was not set up to remind me of it every time I passed two hundred or more handicapped signs as I went down most any street. Life moved forward for me.

Parents of other handicapped children write to me. They ask what I did to succeed. I tell them what I've told you in this chapter. I give them this prescription for the highest chance of their children's success: raise them as loved children instead of raising them as if they were their loved but disabled children. I tell the fathers to buy baseballs and bicycles for their sons and daughters. I tell the mothers to teach their children how to read and write. Maybe your child won't learn to read. Maybe your child won't play soccer. Stephen Hawking describes how he was never good at sports and his motor neurone disease and amyotrophic lateral sclerosis progressed until he was left confined to a wheelchair, a paraplegic, unable to speak. He went on to become the best-known (in some circles, the *only known*) and most brilliant theoretical physicist in history.

Teach them at home if you want to magnify their capabilities. Homeschooling parents find out quickly that it's even easier to teach some children how to read than it was to teach them toilet training.[4] You will multiply the chance for your children's success a hundred times over if you keep them away from the ADA-approved special service workers that hide in the dark corners of public school yards and lurk behind closed classroom doors.

A handicapped child growing up with schools and leaders telling her she cannot make it without their special treatment will have lower self-respect. The handicapped community has a difficult time building up its self-respect because it's told from its first days in school and even earlier sometimes by psychologists and social workers that it cannot succeed without government services and financial handouts. Thus the handicapped community in general struggles today with self-respect as it is told that it is incapable and incompetent and can only succeed in an accommodated world. Without the ADA, the handicapped would be better off financially and morally than they are today.

Every disabled child in school means big bucks. The more services that child gets, the more the bucks flow. Don't let government strangers use your child as their five-year-old little profit generator. That is perhaps my strongest advice to you.

The most important developmental input you can give your child is to make all kinds of activities available to him or her. Do this for those normal and not-so-normal children. Instill self-esteem by teaching them how to read, write, play ball, play the piano, or whatever they show interest in. If you assume they are different, though, they will be. My parents enrolled me in the local Art Linkletter Tap Dancing School when I was five. They got me the shoes and I went. I did fine, but if I had not, they wouldn't have forced me.

Do not first assume abilities or disabilities for your child—and I don't care how severe the handicap may seem to outsiders. Everybody is disabled in something. Just don't expect your children to keep tap dancing when they turn six; if they are boys and have lots of friends, I can attest, they will demand to quit. This chapter's opening account of the psychologist who rudely confronted me about my hands reveals this. Most four-year-olds are taught to be more polite to strangers than she was to me. Her disability was the shameless assumption that anyone handicapped is a victim looking for someone to blame. I am thankful that my mother was not sitting at the table.

4

GOOD INTENTIONS AND UNINTENDED CONSEQUENCES

You, an employer, ask your delivery woman who happens to be white to deliver an invoice across town. A man who happens to be black pulls her out of the car, and she gets hurt.

When she recovers, she informs you that she now has a disability which sends her into panic attacks whenever she sees a black person. Citing the ADA and implying a potential lawsuit, she declares that you must separate her from all black employees and customers.

John Casey, writing in the University of Puget Sound Law Review, *declares this scenario's conclusion: If you refuse her, you are guilty under the ADA and face litigation and immense financial burdens. If you agree with her, you are guilty under the Civil Rights Act and face litigation and immense financial burden.*[1]

W hen discussing the vast gray area of the Americans with Disabilities Act, *Investor's Business Daily*'s John Merline describes how ADA requirements can very well conflict with other workplace laws such as the Family and Medical Leave Act and parts of the National Labor Relations Act.[2] By trying to adhere to one law's requirements, an employer can violate those of another. What makes matters worse is that the EEOC is known to judge complaints on an individual, case-by-case basis. Companies cannot determine from precedent how the EEOC will treat their actions.

In a classic Catch-22, owners of Denver's *Barolo* restaurant learned how it feels to be caught between the ADA and another regulation when they attempted to make their business ADA-compliant as per the Justice Department's orders. The Denver city government required eight and a half months of red tape before the ADA changes could be made. But the Justice Department fined the owners because they did not move faster on the construction in spite of the fact that Denver wouldn't allow the changes to be made sooner due to its own permit-approval delays.[3] (Joseph Heller, call your office.)

LOVE BOMBS AND EARLY PROPAGANDA

The Americans with Disabilities Act is often referred to as a law with good intentions. Even its detractors have said that. Upon closer analysis of its history, however, its well-intentioned foundation begins to look suspect.

Making the ADA into a law during a time when America was not treating the handicapped with disdain required some positioning. The advocates would need to change people's perception of handicapped people from survivors into victims to generate sympathy for the cause. And so a major campaign began immediately to portray the handicapped as victims. Interestingly, today ADA proponents frown on the term *victim*. The Easter Seals of Southern California makes it clear that "victim" is a label never to be used when discussing disabled people.[4] But words are one thing and reality another; for the early ADA advocates, starting a major campaign to portray the handicapped as victims was imperative.

The conversion of the public's perception of respect and admiration of the handicapped to coercion and guilt trips would be an up-hill climb, a hill worthy of the most solid ADA-required ramps and grab bars. The most detailed account appears in Walter K. Olson's *The Excuse Factory*, an exposé of legal paralysis in the workplace. In his book, Olson describes the difficulty that the ADA faced in the creation of a class of victims who were not treated as victims and *did not consider themselves victims.*

> [F]ewer than half [handicapped people] agree in polls that they are a minority group. . . . Many disabled persons are also loath to impose on others. . . . Oppressed minorities are supposed to be persecuted, but the disabled were being love-bombed. In one survey 92 percent of those polled said they felt admiration when they met a severely disabled person. Hire-the-handicapped preferences were considered just fine by most.[5]

But the disability-act proponents had a way around the love-bombing. They felt no hesitation when generalizing about normal people (another term to be avoided around the disabled according to the Easter Seals in Southern California) but were wholly intolerant if someone generalized about the disabled. The activists were particularly forceful in explaining that being sympathetic and favorable to the disabled as a group fails "to recognize them as fully human."[6]

Joseph Shapiro, former writer for *U.S. News & World Report* and now a National Public Radio correspondent, explains that if you view the disabled as inspirational then you are being oppressive towards them.[7] In other words, one damages the disabled by admiring them. (Given that logic, shouldn't we immediately close all state-funded museums so that their artifacts can be protected from admiring patrons?) Shapiro even wrote a book, *No Pity: People with Disabilities Forging a New Civil Rights Movement,* which won several awards from major disability organizations who directly benefit from strengthening the ADA. If you rob Peter to pay Paul, Paul rarely complains.

Olson describes how the *University of Pennsylvania Law Review* further explains this oppression of the disabled when someone admires their overcoming achievements: "Any atmosphere of sympathy is only alleged and apparent and indeed a problem that must be overcome if equality is to be gained."[8] Therefore, if someone shows sympathy to a handicapped person, that sympathy is phony and is only alleged sympathy.

Follow the activists' general strategy to pass the ADA:

1. They needed to turn the disabled into victims.

2. The disabled didn't consider themselves victims.

3. Americans were sympathetic toward the handicapped.

4. Non-disabled Americans already admired and hired the handicapped.

5. The activists would strive to convince Americans that admiration and sympathy were negative attitudes that made disabled people less than human.

In other words, it was the activists themselves who considered the disabled less than fully human. They said the disabled engendered sympathy and were admired so that made them subhuman. If this five-step strategy was not a written, planned, predetermined strategy, it quickly became the de facto one they adopted—with the addition of point 6: *Pass Go, and collect far more than $200.*

According to Olson, pro-ADA activists pointed out that Franklin D.

Roosevelt could only have been elected because the public was unaware that he was wheelchair-bound with poliomyelitis. They also suggested that blind Milton, blind Homer, and the deaf Beethoven's disabilities are seldom considered important when discussing their accomplishments. Deafness strikes me as being an important consideration when speaking about the best-known composer in history. Stephen Hawking cannot walk, move his legs, maneuver his arms, use his hands, or speak. Should not those details be considered useful information when gauging his accomplishments, which include authoring nearly two hundred scientific research papers and a physics book that sold an astounding 9 million copies?[9] Hawking is one of the few theoretical physicists known widely and lauded outside his field—principally because of his brilliance and achievements despite his tremendous disabilities.

TWO KINDS OF CIVIL RIGHTS LEGISLATION

Edward L. Hudgins has written at length about various kinds of civil rights. Traditional racial-based civil rights legislation requires little real financial cost or action. Allowing minorities into establishments where they were not formerly allowed, for example, requires no change in building structures or direct financial costs. Public facilities incur no additional costs when opening their doors to all races. In other words, Hudgins explains how positive actions were not generally required by traditional civil rights legislation.[10]

If the Americans with Disabilities Act is a civil rights act, as it's been called from the beginning, then it is different from its older civil rights cousin. The ADA demands positive and costly actions. A business that is not ADA-compliant must spend money and possibly hire new employees to adhere strictly to the ADA. Home delivery where none existed before is a possible requirement, entrances where none were originally designed may need to be added, and counter heights may need to be changed. Only then is a business getting closer to the ADA's adherence. Even then, given the ADA's inconsistent past litigation, a business never fully knows when or if it is ever compliant.

While the ADA requires both specific and vague actions to reach compliance, it does not feel the need to provide funds for such mandates. State and local government agencies, transportation services, schools, and libraries are required to comply with the ADA but are rarely given the budgets for compliance. For private businesses, costs are far greater than that of a government agency which can spread those costs over the entire community. When the Department of Justice involves itself in an ADA lawsuit, it sues for its own exorbitant fines as well as for other damages. Such selfish use of government power was recognized as far back in America's history as 150 years ago when Frederic Bastiat called similar measures *legal plunder*.[11]

A civil rights law that removes restrictions is far less costly than one that adds them. Businesses must add a specific number of accessible parking spaces to the front of their lots. The ADA thus restricts businesses from being able to design their own parking lots the way they think will benefit customers best. This restriction is especially costly to paid parking lots and garages where each space is a possible income-generator. By reserving an ADA-imposed number of spaces, those parking businesses find these spaces hardly ever filled and even if every other space is full, nobody but those with the mark of the chair can park there. So the spaces remain empty much of the time. And non-disabled customers must pay more to cover these losses.

I have already shown you how the ADA discriminates against the handicapped. But the ADA also harms the non-handicapped. Even if you accept the ADA's grossly inflated figure that 43 million Americans are disabled, then upon inspection you must conclude that the ADA discriminates against the other 220 million Americans. The ADA discriminates against the majority of Americans, and it is that majority of Americans who must pay the ADA's financial damages.

If the ADA did not hamstring a business, then that business could install as many handicapped spaces where it wanted them to go based on its own personal assessment of the community it serves. Such a business could provide these spaces but allow the non-disabled to park in them if all the other spaces in the lot were full. ADA advocates are intolerant to such reasonable plans.

Today's disabled parking spaces are not just marked for the disabled; they also implicitly state that non-disabled cannot park there. It is fine for the ADA to discriminate against normal people. But if a business posted signs on all of its non-disabled spaces showing a wheelchair symbol with a red slash through it, telling the disabled they were not allowed to park in spaces designated for the non-handicapped, heads would roll. Yet the ADA tells this to the non-disabled. As a man with handicaps, I find it distasteful that the government has restricted a set of parking spaces up front where I can park, but it is illegal for my neighbor to do so. Such a rule is embarrassing and makes it more difficult to appear in public when handicapped. Let me state with full disclosure that I have used handicapped parking spaces in my lifetime. It is not the designated space that is distasteful but that the government mandates the designated space and forces people who cannot park there to pay for them.

As long as I bear the mark, better known as a permit hanging from my rearview mirror, I could lace up my roller blades once I park my car in one of those coveted handicapped spots and sail past three police officers who would and could do nothing because I have the permit. Or I could just run around my car twice before racing my neighbor to the front door in a foot race that I'd probably win because he has to park so much farther away than I do. People who support such lunacy as the ADA often care far more about the rules and regulations than results. As long as I follow the rules, it's fine if I take advantage of the result.

If you grew up hearing that everybody is equal under the law, you must have grown up in the Cayman Islands or Tonga or a handful of other nations where such a notion seems to be still true because the ADA has made sure that such a statement is untrue for America. The disabled are far more "equal" than other Americans.

JANICE'S STORY

A woman I know named Janice, a single mother, pulled into a handicapped parking space one morning. She got out of her car and heard yelling. Janice, a joyful, vibrant lady was surprised to see that she herself was the target of the shouts.

The shrieking voice grew shrill: "How dare you park in that handicapped space!" "You don't need to park there!" "What gives *you* the right to park there?"

When Janice indicated the handicapped parking placard hanging from her rearview mirror, the abuse only increased.

Janice is not one to participate in a yelling match. She just walked around to the other side of her car and went about her business. Her business for the next few minutes required the unlatching of her severely handicapped, precious little daughter's special seat so that she then could attach that seat to the base of her daughter's wheelchair that she unfolded and set up. Getting her daughter safely positioned outside the car took about ten minutes every time she did it.

How many truly handicapped families have received this kind of treatment? I would suspect many have. The Americans with Disabilities Act's inconsistencies do little more than provoke hatred and divisiveness in such situations. Those on the political Left often say that one cannot legislate morality. Given that morality and immorality are mutually exclusive, you must conclude that left-leaning, socialistic legislation is thus immoral. A law that engenders such fierce and negative emotion hints at just such immorality. Empty handicapped spaces in an otherwise filled-to-capacity parking lot cause resentment. The worst part of that resentment is consciously or unconsciously aimed at the handicapped. Emotions flare that never would have existed without the ADA.

When a law requires multi-thousands of dollars to be spent for a newly-defined compliance, the government has just taken property away from private citizens once more. A restaurant that must spend $80,000 to comply has $80,000 less to stay competitive and remain in business.

Would things be different if businesses were allowed to adopt whatever accessible changes they wanted, based on their own clientele and based on their own budget constraints? What if businesses were allowed the freedom to design parking lots however they chose? Would they want to reserve any spaces for the handicapped? If they did, would the public be less apprehensive and emotional about those spaces?

Although we'll never be fortunate enough to know what a non-ADA America in the future would look like, Llewellyn H. Rockwell, Jr., paints a vivid picture of what could happen if freedom and sanity were once again returned:

> Who hasn't damned the empty disabled parking slots that pockmark the country thanks to the feds? In contrast, a sign placed by private enterprise at my local grocery store—in pretty pink and blue, adorned with a stork—reserves a space for expectant mothers and engenders feelings of benevolence.[12]

Rockwell goes on to explain that it is illegal for such expectant mothers to park in the handicapped spaces. They don't have the permit to do so.

THE AMERICANS WITHOUT DISABILITIES ACT

Richard D. Holihan testified in a pretrial deposition that he had no disability, past or present. The Ninth U.S. Circuit Court of Appeals stated that under the ADA, Holihan could continue with his trial as though he were disabled—even though he was not disabled.[13]

Holihan was a manager for Lucky Foods, a supermarket chain. In one three-month period, he was accused of manhandling, verbally harassing, and treating his employees with abuse. After Holihan denied any problems, Lucky supermarkets transferred Holihan to a different location. Within the three months that followed, employees filed fifty-one complaints against Holihan of hostility and abuse that included throwing food on the floors when enraged and telling employees to clean up the messes.

Lucky's officials offered Holihan a leave of absence so he could accept counseling from the company's Employee Assistance Program (EAP). Holihan took his leave of absence and began the counseling. His counselor diagnosed him as having "stress-related problems precipitated by work."[14]

During his six-month leave of absence from the Lucky stores, Holihan requested, and got, three additional leaves of absence. Holihan needed the extra time because the two businesses he started took up to eighty hours a week. His sign-making business needed attention as did his new real estate license. Surely holding open houses and getting listings would be far more difficult if Holihan went back to work at Lucky stores too soon. Lucky's management reasonably decided that they would stop extending Holihan's leave of absence as he had gone past the company's six-month leave of absence limit.

The story should have ended there.

Six months later, Holihan returned to Lucky supermarkets and asked for a job. No management positions were available, but the store offered to hire Holihan as a clerk and allow him to apply for management when such a position opened up. Holihan refused that employment offer and went looking for the nearest district court. His complaint stated that the Lucky supermarkets discriminated against him on the basis of his disability.

As this section's opening paragraph indicated, Holihan testified in a pre-trial deposition that he was not disabled and had never been disabled.[15] The court ruled that he was not disabled, and they supplied the reason: Holihan worked his businesses while on the leave of absence.

The story should have ended there.

The court went on to say that the ADA prohibits discrimination against people "regarded as" having a handicap. In other words, the counseling sessions indicated that the Lucky stores regarded Holihan as handicapped even though he was not handicapped. Therefore, the case would move forward.

Considering Holihan's abusive actions at the Lucky store he managed and the results of the court's ruling, it appears that this case disputes the EEOC's Chairman Gilbert Casellas who states that the ADA "does not require employers to tolerate violence from an employee."[16] Casellas then proudly points out that 28 percent of accommodations cost less than $1,000 to implement. He failed to account just how much over $1,000 the other 72 percent of accommodations cost each and every required organization to implement.

Holihan's case is one of the most infamous in the ADA's short history of massive litigation stories. The story strongly implies that if you are a good enough actor to convince your employer that you are disabled, you can sue as though you are disabled when things don't go your way. If the ADA applies to those with disabilities *and* the ADA applies to those without disabilities, who is left to pay the bill?

TROUBLES, RIGHT HERE IN RIVER CITY

Back troubles comprise one of the most frequent ADA complaints, accounting for anywhere from 20 percent to almost 50 percent of physical ADA filings depending on the year studied. The problems generally attributed to the handicapped such as vision, hearing, and mobility limitations comprise only 14 percent of ADA filings. Understandably, unseen ailments such as back pain and emotional problems seem to generate the most friction in ADA battles. Employers find that they cannot address the issue of whether or not the employee is truly disabled. Instead, they must defend as if the employee were.[17]

William Bolte, a handicapped-rights activist, explains a related phenomenon: "The most frequent employment complaint under the ADA is from those already employed *who only discover that they are disabled* when facing dismissal or passed over for promotion."[18]

When discussing the Americans with Disabilities Act, Rockwell points out that not all who claim a disability are faking that disability and recommends a procedure that might give you an indication of who may have physical troubles and who may just be faking. He suggests that you stand on the corner of a busy mall and wave five one-hundred dollar bills in your hand as you yell, "If anyone has back trouble, this money is yours." From the resulting takers, you might have enough data to estimate the number who truly had troubles and the number who took the cash disingenuously. Before going to the mall, he recommends that you get a multi-million dollar cash advance from the taxpayers' coffers before you begin so you don't run out of money too early in the day.[19]

COMPARING LARGE AND SMALL TOWNS

One of the endless problems of the Americans with Disabilities Act is its failure to define disability and who needs to comply. "Is disabled" seems to depend on what "is" is. ADA advocates are quick to point out that the original definition of disabled was loose but that definition has changed in the years since. Has it ever! Officially, the term certainly has gone through changes, but the case-by-case nature of each court decision still implies a gross inconsistency in the law's interpretation a decade and a half after its genesis.

One change has been to reduce the size a company must be to comply. If you wonder if your business is large enough to require compliance, you're much safer to assume that it is. And yet if you bypass the major highways of America and drive through small towns, you could very well drive through entire population centers without seeing one wheelchair space. I have eaten at many a small-town bustling café that employs enough people to require compliance, and yet they have given absolutely no thought to remodeling.

Yet if the next small town happens to have a McDonald's that employs fewer employees than that first café, the McDonald's will have done what they can to meet compliance. It's not that the McDonald's management cares any more or less about the disabled. It's that McDonald's has deep pockets. Water flows downhill, but lawsuits flow up: up to the highest dollar balance available.

A law that applies only to rich companies and not to poor ones is a bad law. The ADA and its proponents do not seem to consider the handicapped important if they are poor, if they live in poorer small towns, or if they patronize poor and small companies. I do not mean to state here that the ADA should apply to all small businesses. It is my point that if the government will not enforce a law for all businesses, then the law should be abolished. Policy shouldn't be determined by the relative "shakedown" factor.

PRODUCERS: SCREEN THOSE CALLERS BETTER

National Public Radio's *Diane Rhem Show* celebrated the ADA's 10-year anniversary in 2000.[20] The guests were Sue Messenger from the Society for Human Resource Management, Rebecca Ogle, the former Executive Director for the Presidential Taskforce on Employment of Adults with Disabilities, and Dick Thornburgh, a former U.S. attorney general. Lynn Neary was guest-hosting for Diane Rhem. The show's tone clearly indicated a celebratory acceptance of the Americans with Disabilities Act. The guests' primary concern focused on how much more work still needed to be done to strengthen the ADA.

Eventually the panelists took phone calls. Edmundo, from Dallas, Texas, was the first caller. He blindsided the panelists right off the bat by announcing that he was, in fact, blind. (Incidentally, he was the only one on the show who used that direct term. The show's host and studio panelists who were not blind—physically, that is—seemed to me to be embarrassed that he used this term instead of the more euphemistic *vision-impaired*.) Edmundo first declared how the Americans with Disabilities Act has cost him money, cost his family money, and harmed his children. He then stated how he'd once heard Walter Williams, a nationally prominent black economist, discuss how thrilled he was that he grew up, was educated, and was married before the Civil Rights act was passed. Edmundo said he was glad that he grew up before the ADA. I sat there astounded as déjà vu came over me when he said those very things that I've said for over a decade. The host's and panelists' silence was deafening as he continued.

Edmundo told of his small business that he started in 1994. A man applied for a job. The man was, in Edmundo's own words, "a drug-addicted, AIDS-infected homosexual." Edmundo, showing wisdom and good stewardship, did not hire the applicant so the applicant hired a lawyer. The resulting lawsuit cost Edmundo a large amount of money just to prepare for the case then eventually to appear in court with representation after all the preparation. Edmundo did not go into depth about the toll on his personal and business life, but, obviously, the situation was severely costly for him and his family in many ways.

His family was understandably distraught over the situation as well. What is more frightening than being hauled into court to the threat of an overwhelming lawsuit?

Ann Reesman, general counsel for the Equal Employment Advisory Counsel (EEAC) says that just getting a "garden-variety [ADA] case dismissed" costs from $50,000 to $100,000 in attorney fees alone.[21] The charges brought against Edmundo could very well extend beyond what might be considered garden-variety to reach severe levels. Under Title III, the Department of Justice can impose a $50,000 civil penalty for a first violation and $100,000 for subsequent violations. After those civil damages, plaintiffs usually add punitive damage requests to such suits as well.

All this cost Edmundo time away from family and business, and he became distraught with worry about the whole situation. When Edmundo walked into the courtroom with his white cane, the judge saw he was blind and declared that a lawsuit alleging Edmundo would discriminate against the handicapped was a frivolous lawsuit and wisely tossed out the case. Edmundo did not seem thrilled; the fact that his side won the case didn't restore him. He did not receive his expenses back and could not recover the time he lost during the preparations for the courtroom scene.

Before the on-air guests could gather their thoughts and respond, Edmundo went on to describe how the ADA damaged his children by requiring them to be in "mainstream" classrooms. In its most pure form, mainstreaming is the act of placing all levels of students in the same class, whereby some may be intellectually gifted and some may be severely retarded. The school slowed down Edmundo's children's education in those classes so that the slower students could better compete with the advanced students. The end result was that the slower students got the same halting education they would have gotten in a separate classroom environment while the more advanced students were taught less than they would otherwise have been taught. Edmundo had to hire private tutors so that his children could be educated at the level they required, which cost him more money.

This phone call seemed to set a tone that was not planned for this National Public Radio broadcast. The panelists on the show responded by downplaying Edmundo's concerns. They promptly thanked him for the call and hung up on him before making any comments, effectively preventing any kind of dialogue. Dick Thornburg explained that he had a child with mental challenges who was placed in regular classrooms and how beneficial it was for the rest of the class to see that a disabled person can be productive. (In so stating, he went against the ADA's founders who dislike admiration for the disabled.) He went on to describe how Edmundo and others like him ignore this benefit of mainstreaming. This response completely disregarded Edmundo's complaint. If anything it emphasizes his argument against mainstreaming. It is obviously detrimental to the more advanced students' education to be taught at the slower level, and yet Thornburg thinks the more advanced students benefited by the mere fact they saw a disabled child learn.

Larry Elder, an L.A.-area radio host and nationally syndicated columnist, received a letter from Mary Blanton in 2001 that is rather telling, not unlike Edmundo's story.[22] She describes how she was born with a rare genetic deletion that rendered her legally blind. All her life others told her that she should rely on the welfare state for sustenance. She sarcastically (and accurately) points out that it appears the disabled in America should not be expected to support themselves. She then explains what she does for a living. Instead of taking from others she is a successful software engineer. Some have actually told her that she threatens other people's benefits from the welfare state because she supports herself and is committed to her career.

Mary adds this:

> I could be the poster child for the welfare state. Instead, I am the
> poster child for what the "disabled" can do if they want to. The

more I hear about victimhood, about the Social Safety Net, about how the government owes people a life and a living, about how the government should provide a retirement plan for us, the more I talk about my "disability." I do this in the vain hope that one other person with a disability will rise to the challenge and take responsibility for their own life and living.

ARE THEY DISABLED OR NOT?

The ongoing debate over the term disabled started during the ADA's inception and has proved problematic ever since. On the NPR-broadcasted 10-year anniversary celebration, the former U.S. Attorney General attempted to clarify the meaning of disabled. He explained that a legal definition is based on, "the inability of an individual to participate in a major life activity or perceived as being able to, meaning that they cannot be treated differently as though they had a disability." Such definitions cause all sorts of problems, at least for defendants over the years. The ADA often states a requirement of *reasonable accommodation* which commonly seems to mean one must make every accommodation possible and do virtually anything requested by an employee. At the same time, one is not supposed to be overt in making an accommodation for someone who is termed disabled. Doing so violates the ADA by not protecting the privacy of the disabled.

As Sue Messenger explained on the show, using the term "accommodation" can violate the EEOC's guidelines for the disabled when applied to workers who may be disabled due to depression. The term "accommodation" might give other employees a hint that this employee is depressed. This opens up a new can of worms in the ADA. Such censorship forces a return to the debate of what constitutes a disability. Pro-ADA advocates insist without question that depression falls under the category of being a disability. Whether depression is disabling is *not* a debate I am making here. But the danger of putting unseen problems under the umbrella of a disability is that such problems are easily claimed by those who want to take advantage. Too many benefits are awarded in ADA lawsuits that encourage people to adopt unseen problems.

Messenger went on to explain that with other civil rights-based laws, such as those regarding race or sex, it's very easy to determine the status of the accusing party. After all, it's not difficult to discern if one is African American or female. When you're dealing with the ADA, it's more challenging, says Messenger: "people with disabilities come in groups of one." Each individual case has to be weighed against the rights of the employer. Sadly, when an employer has a question about compliance, 81 percent of employers turn to attorneys. Generally human resource departments don't have to turn to attorneys in such high percentages to get simple questions answers in other kinds of cases.

A Florida Subcommittee on the Constitution, chaired by Charles T. Canady, exposes the fact that turning to attorneys can get you into further legal problems:

> The Subcommittee is conducting this hearing today because of concerns that the progress brought about by the ADA is being threatened by a growing number of lawyers who are generating large sums in legal fees for pointing out often simple fixes that would bring properties into compliance with the ADA. The lure of large attorneys' fees is so great that attorneys may even settle cases for attractive sums for themselves by agreeing to terms by which a property would not even be fully accessible under the ADA.[23]

Joseph R. Fields wrote to Chairman Canady two days before that subcommittee meeting to help support the Chairman's claim:

> Over the past two years, south Florida Federal and State Courts have been inundated with lawsuits alleging ADA violations. The primary target seems to be small businesses who can ill afford to fight and who eventually are forced to pay their adversaries fees. . . . Last year, I represented a small business owner whose tenant sells baseball cards in the Lake Worth Florida area. Upon

correcting the deficiencies noted in the Plaintiff's complaint, he was then met with a demand for $4,500,000 in attorneys' fees and costs. . . . [I]t became apparent to me that forms were being used over and over again and there was nowhere near $4,500,000 worth of work in that case.[24]

Nice work if you can get it.

In light of Messenger's statement that "people with disabilities come in groups of one," the ADA's founding history seems even more suspect as to whether or not it had good intentions. Walter K. Olson describes the plight of ADA advocates when they began their apparent quest to turn the disabled into victims so the ADA would pass. Olson recounts how no single group of disabled people existed because there was no single disabled identity. There were organizations for the blind, paraplegic, and deaf, for example, but no umbrella handicap group existed that sought benefits that only the ADA provided. Therefore, such a group had to be formed, and the larger the better. Their final number of 43 million disabled in America is quite a group indeed, especially for a group that did not exist until the ADA founders realized they needed exactly such a group of victims to get the ADA's passage:

Any semblance of "disabled nation" unity fell entirely to pieces when other disabling conditions were added to the comparison. Many persons with permanent, stable disabilities get annoyed (and not unreasonably) at the outside world's habit of "medicalizing" their condition, or expecting every paraplegic to pursue a vain struggle to walk rather than get on with life. Soon, however, it was announced that all the conditions requiring the greatest medical intervention and personal effort to fight—cancer, heart disease, contagious diseases such as tuberculosis—counted as disabilities, too. So did alcoholism and drug abuse (even if they'd been conquered and the person had been sober for years), as well as mental disorders.[25]

The ADA founders had ample help from both political parties, neither of which wanted to be viewed as opposing the disabled. The government expansion of George Bush, Sr.'s administration now, in retrospect, produced the subsequent ADA's enormous cost to taxpayers that nobody except the ADA's founders and true conservatives could have foreseen. Helping to seal the ADA's financial tolls, the Bush administration delegated the authoring of the ADA's details to the American Civil Liberties Union. To ensure that the ADA stayed on course, the Bush administration then appointed Evan Kemp, Jr., a former Ralph Nader-funded litigation group official, to be the new EEOC Chairman. To claim a victory for the public, President George Bush compared his Americans with Disabilities Act to the fall of the Berlin Wall.[26]

An overlooked problem with comparing the ADA to the Berlin Wall's fall is that the former engenders a socialistic mindset and imposes devastating costs on its public while the latter eliminates a socialistic mindset and ends devastating costs on its public.

One of the ADA's goals is to allow for the independence of the disabled. You cannot be dependent and independent at the same time. The feminist movement is now combatted by countless female detractors who complain that the independence required by the feminists' actions has set women back and resulted in much unhappiness. But the moment you accept help from someone else, you've given up some of your independence. Reliance on people to help us in any situation is not necessarily a bad thing. Not being able to do something due to an inability or disability is nothing to be ashamed of. But the ADA acts as though it's something to be ashamed of when they require employers to refrain from using the word "accommodation" around any employee who is disabled because others might hear they are disabled. Asking for help is an honorable request, and when someone responds to that call for help then humanity benefits. Self-imploding ADA requirements such as not being able to act like you're accommodating when you accommodate creates tremendous friction in the world. Even worse, this friction hampers the ability and desire of one person to help another.

EQUALITY FOR ALL MEANS EQUALITY FOR NONE

The ADA anniversary panel on NPR's *Diane Rhem Show* unintentionally exposed many problems. One of the panelists, Rebecca Ogle, the former Executive Director for the Presidential Taskforce on Employment for Adults with Disabilities, had this to say in the law's support: "The ADA is a civil rights statute and not an employment statute. . . . 54 million disabled people can now participate in employment opportunities, in state and local government, in all public accommodations, in telecommunications, and transportation."[27]

First of all, the ADA has been abused to the point of absurdity time and time again on employment-related cases. The result is that the Americans with Disabilities Act *is* an employment statute. They can call it whatever they like, but it's used primarily as an employment-abuse tool. Secondly, I'm unsure where she found 11 million more disabled over the 43 million that the ADA's founders discovered just ten years earlier. Nevertheless, it is the rest of her statement that troubles me. Such a statement is an offense to the thousands and thousands of truly disabled people who worked in those very areas for years before the ADA. Those individuals also participate since the ADA's passage, but now their employers live in constant fear of the courts.

Ogle seemed overly stern when she then said, "A lot of businesses have taken the attitude of wait and see, wait and see if they'll get sued. We need to send a strong message that the adoption of that attitude will not be accepted!" She declares that it is the disabled person's civil right to equal accommodations. However, employers are really put-upon with these kinds of thoughts-turned-legalities. Return once more to the illegality of the term *accommodation* as it may signal to other workers that an employee is depressed. No quadriplegic ever required privacy so that people would not and could not be able to notice that he was a quadriplegic. If depression is a true disability then why do ADA advocates act ashamed that it is?

A law cannot create a forced equality where none existed previously; any law that attempts to do such a thing will do exactly the opposite. It will teach those who might be able to take advantage of the law to do that instead of using their own abilities.

In that NPR broadcast, Dick Thornburgh reflected on ADA's origin. Restating the newly-conjured 54 million disabled figure, he described how "a critical mass formed from advocacy groups to wrap all this together [the ADA] into one package." This history doesn't seem to correlate well to actual history as Walter K. Olson sees it, which I described earlier in this chapter where ADA advocates had to work very hard to form a disabled group large enough to justify what was about to be thrust on America. But then again, in that same set of remarks Thornburgh declares with a completely straight face that the Americans with Disabilities Act "doesn't rely on preferences for persons with disabilities."

He then says, "A very loose definition of the ADA [disabled] was included in the ADA." He said this was to make it flexible. History has proved just how flexible—or better, *arbitrary*—the ADA is.

5

SPREADING THE BURDEN:
The ADA in the Workplace

Since we have yet to establish employment quotas for the disabled, a shrewd employer simply avoids hiring anyone who might trigger this bottomless pit of legal demands.
—American Spectator, January 1998

Whenever possible, employers tend to shun disabled employees, which is why even the official figures reveal a higher unemployment rate among authentically disabled people than before the act passed. Because of the mandate that endlessly escalating "accommodations" be provided, and that these costs not be paid at the expense of the employee's salary, disabled employees are far costlier to hire than before. (For example, the EEOC says that an employee with no hands must be accommodated with another employee to provide manual dexterity.) Moreover, disabled people are perceived as walking lawsuits.
—LLEWELLYN H. ROCKWELL, JR.,
"The ADA," Ludwig von Mises Institute, May 16, 2003.

Walking lawsuits—what an embarrassment the Americans with Disabilities Act has been for truly disabled people.

While much of *Disabling America* touches on the ADA's impact on businesses, this chapter focuses specifically on business. The reason the business world's impact is so critical is because every transaction you make, from Wal-Mart to Nordstrom's, and every time you get your car repaired and your prescription filled, the Americans with Disabilities Act has damaged the business you are interacting with. That damage is not always direct through abusive litigation—often the damage is indirect. For example, higher building costs can translate into higher costs for the products and services that you must pay for. In addition, the very jobs you seek may be fewer due to the ADA's impact, and this chapter focuses quite a bit on the ADA's employment ramifications.

SUCCESS: BY WHAT DEFINITION?

You should not look for the Americans with Disabilities Act's success in isolated cases. Anecdotal evidence simply cannot justify the positive or negative aspects of any program even though a continued pattern of anecdotal evidence, such as the fraud generated by the ADA lawsuits, certainly should be an indicator that something is amiss. The most important question to be asked should be this: How well has the Americans with Disabilities Act done one of its primary jobs in providing employment for the handicapped?

An indication of how many handicapped are currently employed is certainly one strong measure of the ADA's success. The Cato Institute's Edward L. Hudgins tells how the number of on-the-job legal complaints from those traditionally thought of as truly disabled—the deaf, blind, and wheelchair users—has decreased.[1] So perhaps the ADA has been successful at happily employing more of these individuals. The sad truth is that the decrease is probably because businesses have hired fewer handicapped employees. Hudgins explains that the National Organization of the Disabled claims only 31 percent of the working-aged persons with disabilities were employed as of December 1993, compared to 33 percent in 1986, four years before President George Bush, Sr., signed the ADA into law.

Lew Rockwell quotes similar statistics and describes that the downtrend for hiring the disabled has continued into the present:

> From 1986 to 1991, two years after the ADA went into law, unemployment among the mildly disabled went down slightly (14.8 to 12.4 percent). But among the moderately and severely disabled, unemployment went up from 21.4% to 27.9%. Looking at a longer string of data through 1994, workforce participation rates went slightly down among men (from 60% to 58%) and slightly up among women. In 1986, 66% of unemployed people with disabilities wanted work but couldn't find it. Today, 79% of them can't find work.
>
> It's remarkable to realize that the flat-to-falling trend for disability employment . . . occurred during the economic boom of the 1990s. Only bad law like the ADA can accomplish something like that.[2]

Rockwell goes on to explain that government payments to the disabled (Supplemental Security Income) increased from 4.2 million in 1989 to 6.8 million people after the turn of the century. He makes a good case that businesses are terrified of hiring the disabled. Rockwell clearly understands the ADA's impact when he describes how the most efficient way to eliminate the disabled from the workforce is for the government to insist that they be treated just as the non-disabled; then they won't be hired. Rockwell explains, "Fire [the handicapped] or fail to promote them, and they could cost you hundreds of thousands in legal expenses."

Who can blame businesses for their lack of desire to hire the handicapped? The ADA tosses any notion of employee efficiency out the window. The ADA is almost a perfect definition of the Law of Unintended Consequences at work.

MCDONALD'S IS FAT-FREE

No doubt you've heard of the woman who sued McDonald's because her coffee was hot and she spilled it on her lap. Another McDonald's suit took place in April of 2003 that did not generate nearly the same amount of publicity. I suspect the lower attention was because the ADA seems to be a protected regulation that nobody wants to expose out of fear of looking anti-handicapped. But the case makes clear the absurdity of the ADA.

A New Haven, Connecticut, man claimed that McDonald's did not hire him because he is overweight. He weighs in at 420 pounds. His suit states that McDonald's violated the Americans with Disabilities Act. For an added edge, he listed the Connecticut Fair Employment Practices Act in the suit as a defendant also.[3] The man alleged that his obesity problem makes him disabled. Indeed, accuracy was never a goal of the ADA, and the term *disabled* allows the ADA to wield their power more than the term *handicapped* would. The man said his disability was why McDonald's decided not to hire him. McDonald's took the obvious defense that unless obesity can be linked to some physiological disorder then the obesity does not physically impair under the definitions of the ADA. Therefore McDonald's asked the judge to dismiss the case.

United States District Judge Stefan R. Underhill, in an increasingly predictable response, refused to dismiss the case and said the case will go to trial. Whatever conclusion is reached, the fact that the ADA was involved strongly suggests that a thirty-nine-cent hamburger may now be a thing of the past for the citizens of New Haven, Connecticut.

&

MCDONALD'S CAN'T REFUSE THE ADA'S COMEUPPANCE

The fact that McDonald's was designated as one of the "Top 50 Companies for Disabled Workers" from Careers & disABLED magazine is completely forgotten when someone sues McDonald's under the ADA. I suspect that in such cases the defense is barred from discussing that important fact.

DIRTY HARRY AND DIRTY LAWYERS

Clint Eastwood owns the Mission Ranch Hotel in Carmel, California. The combination of rich actor and rich businessman was too much for ADA believers to pass up. So Diane zum Brunnen sued Eastwood because his hotel was not fully wheelchair accessible. The room she stayed in was wheelchair accessible, but she was charged $225 while someone else only paid $85 for a room. To compound Eastwood's problems (and compound the dollars sought), his only wheelchair-accessible bathroom in his restaurant was two hundred feet from the actual eating area, across a parking lot. In addition, his main office could only be reached by stairs.[4] As Myles Kantor points out, Eastwood used a discretionary rate system to cover his costs. Discretionary simply means Eastwood charged what he thought was best as the owner of the hotel. The plaintiff seemed to think "discretionary" meant "discriminatory."

Clint Eastwood refused to settle the case. He said, "In my opinion, you settle when you're wrong." Using words that I would never dream of saying (in print), Eastwood also stated, "It's a racket. The typical thing is to get someone who is disabled in collusion with sleazebag lawyers, and they file suits." Unbelievably, the jury found Eastwood guilty of all charges but refused to award any financial damages to the plaintiff. In other words, Eastwood was out what was certainly huge trial-preparation costs but did not have to pay zum Brunnen one cent.

Can we hope that future juries will reach these kinds of fiscally-responsible decisions? History doesn't suggest that outcome. As one radio host might say, this jury's decision was nothing more than a random act in a mindless legal system.[5]

What makes the Eastwood case stand apart from other legions of lawsuits like it is that the jury allowed for no damages. Yet an unexpected sequel took place some time later that makes that case even more interesting.

One of the attorneys who represented Diane zum Brunnen was himself later sued because his office was not accessible to the disabled! The attorney, Paul Rein, did not have an office bathroom properly accommodating to wheelchair users.[6] (By the way, this is known as not being *wheelchair friendly*, and I am not making that up.) George Louie, Executive Director of the Oakland, California–based Americans with Disabilities Advocates, took Rein to court over this ADA violation. Ironically, Louie was one of Rein's former clients.

One violation was that attorney Paul Rein's bathroom grab bars were inadequate. The plaintiff, George Louie, weighed approximately 300 pounds at the time of the suit's filing.[7] In addition, the toilet was two inches shorter than federal guidelines permit. Not only will the government tell you to remove your round doorknobs but it will also dictate exactly the size and type of toilet you are allowed to install. In an interview, Louie had this to say:

> When you go to sit down on the toilet, you need to position yourself with grab bars. They're not positioned right. The toilet is too close to the wall. It's 16 inches. It should be 18 inches.[8]

When Congress passed the ADA in 1990 and President Bush signed it into law, the rooting press didn't say too much about how you may be hauled into court if your toilets were two inches too close to a wall. That would not have been good publicity.

The defendant, attorney Paul Rein, specializes in disabilities suits. You might note here that Rein's bathroom did have grab bars. Until this case, he made his living representing the disabled. None of his other clients brought forth any suits or had ever complained in any way about Rein's office and facilities. The ADA requests "reasonable accommodations," and Rein seems to have made reasonable accommodations with the grab bars that were in place. Yet in the eyes of business owners, the ADA is rarely reasonable, and Rein was found guilty.

BUSINESSES TRULY ARE LITIGATION TARGETS

George Louie has filed hundreds of lawsuits against California Bay Area businesses for supposed ADA violations. Was Louie actually discriminated against hundreds of times or did he seek out these lawsuits? You be the judge of that.

Knowing more about our man Louie sheds light on the darker aspects of the ADA. One would think that he would first expose an ADA violation, request from the business a change to accommodate the ADA by explaining all the benefits that business might reap from the change, and then move on to spread his goodwill and goal for an accommodating America. Perhaps this is exactly what Louie does, but evidence—in the form of hundreds of lawsuits—indicates the contrary.[9]

Louie claims he has targeted "just about every bank in California." He's hit major chains such as Blockbuster and McDonald's and small independents such as local offices and restaurants. In one chunk of suits that began around the year 2000, Louie went after numerous wineries in California's northwest region. One would really have to enjoy the fruit of the vine to innocently stumble (pardon the pun) upon so many ADA-flouting wineries. What makes his visits stranger is that Louie doesn't even drink. He purchased a bottle of wine from each of them to locate all their ADA violations, and he still has the bottles in his home as evidence when needed.[10] If it sounds like a vendetta, it's understandable.

If you're a business owner, Louie's coming to get you. His organization now includes close to twenty lawyers throughout America with offices in Las Vegas, New Orleans, and Seattle. He admits that most of his cases settle out of court. Does this mean that the businesses he sues fix all their violations? The answer is not completely clear in every case, but Louie does say that in each case the business must fix the accommodation violation, pay both sides' attorney fees (it seems that attorney fees are somehow *always* taken care of in ADA cases), and pay the plaintiff, which includes both George Louie himself and his organization.

One would assume that if the violations are fixed in a timely manner then a money settlement for Louie and a money settlement for Louie's organization would be unneeded. Is his goal to achieve accessibility or financial gain? If financial, then ADA opponents are once again vindicated because they warned this would happen even before the ADA's passage in 1990.

Businesses have asked Louie and others for a ninety-day notification. Often, these businesses don't even know they fail to comply with the cryptic and vague ADA regulations because building inspectors and other government officials have approved their buildings. The requested ninety days to reach Louie's stated compliance gives them time to correct any deficiencies before Louie litigates. If they don't comply in those ninety days, then he can go through with the suit. Although this sounds eminently reasonable, it does not sound so to Louie. He refuses to implement such a policy. He goes on to say that businesses should not get ninety days because bank robbers do not get ninety grace periods when caught. Perhaps it is unrelated, but Louie served several stints of prison time from 1968 until 1990 for grand theft, robbery, and other convictions.[11]

REGULATIONS BY THE TRUCKLOAD

What are the chances that the business you patronize, work at, or perhaps own will face an ADA lawsuit? At this point in time, the chances are probably higher for this kind of suit than any other. The reason is that the ADA itself is in many places so cryptic and vague. Vague language makes for arbitrary applications which means the ADA can very easily be applied against anyone at any time.

You may hear that the ADA applies only to businesses of certain sizes. Originally the ADA imposed its rules and regulations only on companies with more than twenty-five employees. After July 26, 1996, companies with fifteen or more employees were brought into the foray. If your company is smaller, you're not out of the woods. To show that even a one-employee pushcart kiosk business in your local mall is not out of the ADA's bull's-eye, here is a quote directly from the U.S Department of Justice: "To meet the goals of the ADA, the law established requirements for private businesses of all sizes."[12]

A person adept at understanding the difference between private and public businesses might very well understand that this statement means there is no longer a truly private business left in America. To the extent that a government controls private businesses of any size, those private businesses are no longer "private," certainly not in the ultimate sense. The more intrusive the control becomes the less private the business can remain. The ADA even dictates how many disabled signs you will have, where you will put them, and at what heights they are to go. (Interestingly, the ADA refuses to call those signs "wheelchair signs," "disabled signs," or heaven forbid, "handicapped signs." The ADA's authors and promoters call those signs "international symbols of accessibility"! Social engineers never use small, simple words and tight, succinct phrases if longer ones will confuse more people.)

To further clarify that all businesses are targets, the Justice Department goes on to say, "If you own, operate, lease, or lease to a business that serves the public, then, you are covered by the ADA and have obligations for existing facilities as well as for compliance when a facility is altered or a new facility is constructed."

The vagueness and contradictory requirements are always a source of concern for anybody who attempts to comply. For example, if a counter is too high then you violate the ADA. If a table is too low then you violate the ADA. All counters with cash registers are to be no higher than thirty-six inches. I would think this helps promote back problems in your taller employees. Perhaps this alone helps keep the ADA alive by eventually adding to the disability rolls. Do we need an ATA for Americans with Tall Abilities?

The real complications arise when you attempt to decipher the ADA's piles of regulations. Decide for yourself whether the following is plain and simple:

> If a 180 degree turn is needed to exit an area, then a 60 inch diameter turning space or a 36 inch wide T is needed. The space for a T turn requires at least 36 inches of width for each segment of the T and it must fit within a 60 inch by 60 inch area.[13]

As asbestos-removal business owners were delighted to learn, it's not just the government and legal profession who can benefit from vague laws. The asbestos-removal industry has been one of the fastest-growing businesses in America as legal asbestos-scare tactics continue to cost American businesses billions of dollars in repair. Now, a new industry of ADA contractors has sprung up to meet the demands of the legal wins against business since the ADA was signed into law. Contractors who specialize in untangling these cryptic, detailed, and seemingly-endless regulations receive the ADA-required remodeling contracts.

Such ambiguous regulations help explain why the United States Department of Justice has over ten thousand pages of material on its Web site directly related to ADA court victories and settlements.[14]

A MILLION REASONS TO SUE

Generally, if an employee is denied employment for an illegal reason, that employee is awarded damages equal to the salary he or she has missed being out of work. Punitive damages may also be added. A Pennsylvania employment case complicates matters somewhat, at least for employers.

Denise Davis, thirty-seven, was allowed to work from home due to her Crohn's disease. Davis is an insurance underwriter. Her employer gave her a flexible schedule to enable her to work from home. After some time, however, the company decided that she needed to spend specific days at the company office for meetings and the like. Davis filed a lawsuit against her employer stating that the employer had reneged on their original deal—one that allowed her to work from home on a flexible schedule without any specific days she had to report to the office. She stated that she was unable to commit to any specific days in the office. She said that she could not predict in advance when her condition might flare up.[15]

The jury awarded Davis almost $1.3 million in estimated economic damages as well as $200,000 in compensatory damages. The considerable size of the award is due to an economist who testified at the trial. The economist stated that while Davis suffered wage losses of only $40,000, no employer is likely to hire her due to her required accommodation. So he estimated Davis' future salary wages through the age of sixty-seven at more than $1.2 million. She received thirty years' worth of pay up front for winning her case.

The economist was all but saying that after this case, whether Davis won or lost, she wouldn't be hired by anyone else, so she deserved damages from her current employer through age sixty-seven. If she wouldn't be hired by other companies due to her disabilities, then at the very least it is those companies that should pay for the wages she wouldn't get *not* working for them and not her current employer. But to assume no one would hire her is a ridiculous assumption. There are many things Davis can do from home to earn a living. (I've worked from home for more than a decade.)

The economist was implying that if the company is guilty of past violations then that company should pay for all future violations by any future company that would deny her employment. Using an economist as a witness is always handy. It's been said that if you ask three economists a question you'll get four answers. The defense should have put its own economist on the witness stand to counteract this one since finding a contradictory economic opinion would be no challenge.

The most troublesome thing to note about this case is its ability to be applied to all other ADA cases. A precedent has been set. In all subsequent ADA cases against employers, plaintiffs need only an economist or some other paid expert witness to testify that if the plaintiff wins then the defendant should be held accountable for all projected earnings until the age of retirement. This addition instantly adds millions of dollars to all ADA-related employment suits—further incentive to sue.

A side consideration to this particular case might be future technology and biotechnology achievements. If a cure for Crohn's disease appears on the market any time soon, or even any time before Davis' retirement, or if advancements are made so that her symptoms disappear, will Davis be required to repay the awarded damages from that point forward because she would then be employable? You know that's not going to happen.

EAT THE RICH

Small towns, as I've pointed out earlier, are less likely to be ADA compliant. Either those small town businesses don't care about the disabled or they know they won't be targets of such suits because they have little money to pay in damages.

George Louie's organization, the Americans with Disabilities Advocates, helps shed some light on why little small town businesses don't yet have to be as afraid of litigious Louie. In an interview, when Louie was asked if he could be more helpful in urging businesses to comply instead of filing suits immediately, he discussed the wineries he was going after. Louie says he would do so in some cases, but not for "these guys who have a million dollar house on the property crying, 'Oh, I'm a mom-and-pop organization!'"[16]

Such statements do make me wonder if Louie only cares about the handicapped who patronize large businesses that pay large settlements and damages awards. Surely that cannot be the case, right?

I would like to know which local, state, and federal buildings Louie has gone into with the express consent of locating their ADA deficiencies and suing them. Since the government generally is immune from such lawsuits (do you ever wonder why the government has such little hesitation in passing these laws?), I suspect Louie has not wasted his time doing so. Time is money you know.

♿

THE REIGNING ADA CHAMPION

In spite of the hundreds of cases that George Louie has brought against companies, it is John D. Mallah, known as the "ADA's Busiest Complaint Filer," who wins the big money from the ADA. The National Law Journal states that "Mallah and his partner have sued at least 740 businesses—car dealerships, fast food franchises, drug stores, run-down motels."[17] Most of these 740 suits were brought on behalf of a disabled-rights group's activist who, coincidentally, is Mallah's uncle.

BEYOND RAMPS AND GRAB BARS

An incredibly angry woman called into NPR's ADA tenth anniversary show to talk about the ADA.[18] As her story unfolds, we learn that she is hearing-impaired and that a university library recently hired her. Once she got to the job, she let her employers know that she needed amplification equipment for the telephone headsets. She did not go into detail on exactly what work she was hired to do, but the work obviously required the use of phones. She was angry because the university took a long time to get the amplification equipment. Perhaps they had not even wanted to supply the equipment in the first place. Perhaps the lag was too long between the time of her hire and the arrival of the amplified headsets.

As a handicapped person I can tell you my immediate response to hearing such a story which some may find shocking: during an interview process, if I need something to do the job that others do not require, I expect to supply that device myself. Depending on the circumstances, my second recourse might be to make my need known during the interview process and let the potential employer decide if the benefits of hiring me outweigh the cost of any special equipment I require.

Why would people apply for a job, be told they have the job, and then not tell of a requirement to do that job until after starting to work for that organization?

In the past when I interviewed for jobs, I wanted my potential employers to know if I had limitations. They did not need to know that I only had one leg so I never told any of them. They couldn't tell I had an artificial leg because it's not something they would be able to determine by watching me walk or run (or rollerblade or ride a bicycle or . . .). But my hands were obvious. A total of three short fingers where ten normally appear is not something that can be kept out of view for long. Being that computers are my specialty, I always applied for computer-related employment, and I would always offer full disclosure that I could only type in the range of forty-five to fifty-five words per minute. I told all employers this during the interview. They would then tell me that only their secretaries typed faster as far as they knew and that they saw no reason for that to be an issue. The point is, I always told them.

I was sad that the caller showed so much anger when describing her situation. She expected her employer to buy devices that would be used only by her, unless subsequent hearing-impaired people were hired later. But, unfortunately, her actions likely make it very difficult for that university to want to hire hearing-impaired people in the future.

Her anger made me think about my situation, which is not too different. Every few years, my artificial leg wears out, and I have to buy a new one. Those legs are not cheap. Every job I've had requires that I walk to my desk somehow. Doesn't *equal access* imply that my employer needs to make sure I'm supplied with two fully-working legs just like all the other employees? Why should I spend the $5,000 to $10,000 required when I need both legs to be equally equipped with all the other workers there? If I were fortunate to have an insurance company that pays some of the charges (I'm not), then why should *my* premiums be affected when the company I work for should buy me one twice a decade? Why should I be out $10,000 for a new leg when the hearing-impaired woman would only be out $100 or less depending on the head-set amplifier she buys (if she had to buy it herself)?

The ADA says it requires only "reasonable accommodations" for businesses' customers and employees. But what does this mean? If it means only less expensive changes are to be made to handle people such as the hearing impaired but not changes that are more costly, such as buying me a new leg, then the ADA neglects those who are extremely handicapped. Of course, I am not arguing that folks like me should be included in such things—quite the contrary. I argue that *nobody* should be covered by the ADA. But the point here is to show how employers are put upon by ADA-enabled individuals. The full power of the United States Department of Justice stands behind these employees when they demand that their employers supply special equipment.

I don't know if the woman asked the university during her job interview whether they had such devices. I have my doubts. If she did, the university should have the ability and the right to decide before hiring her if the added cost of her employment is worth what she can bring to the organization. If not, then she could be told that budget constraints kept them from equipping the phones as she required. She then could determine if the salary from that job made up for the cost she would pay to buy the equipment herself. Obviously, if she did that then she could take that equipment when she left so that she could use the phone at all subsequent places of her employment.

The Americans with Disabilities Act certainly doesn't allow employers freedom to perform a cost-benefit analysis on handicapped employees. The business might be able to use proper financial analysis to make an investment in a product, but when it comes to hiring the handicapped, the government acts as though it knows what is better for the company than the company's founders, analysts, and employees.

What if such an atrocious scenario didn't stop with the demand for special equipment? Private contractors could also use this to their full advantage. After the dot-com bust early this century, companies had to cut back dramatically on high-tech employees. Contract programmers and Web page designers are common. If a contract programmer is hired, the contract for the job and exact payment is agreed upon and signed, then if the contract worker shows up the first day and starts demanding that the company buy devices to make that worker equal with the others, in my view that contract worker has violated his own contract. He or she agreed upon a price, and that price didn't include the cost of amplified headsets, wheelchairs, artificial legs, or whatever that person is demanding. I would say, though, that such a contract worker has little to fear. In today's climate, no employer is going to question such a request if the alternative is a day in court with an ADA lawyer.

Edward L. Hudgins tries to make some sense out of the ADA's "reasonable accommodations" when he writes:

The ADA requires employers to make reasonable accommodations for employees with disabilities. But the specific accommodations mentioned in the act are anything but reasonable. For example, for an employer to provide qualified readers or interpreters—considered "reasonable" under the ADA—without regard to the employee's payscale, can be very costly. The facts indicate that by a cost-benefit standard, Title I has been less than successful [a list of the ADA's principal provisions is listed in this book's Appendix].[19]

Here's the dirty truth: The degree to which an employee can take advantage of the ADA is too often the degree to which it's done. Buying phone amplifiers might cost a maximum of $100 each, so few people worry about the company's position at such a low cost. But once a certain dollar level is reached, whatever that may be, no moral person would consider using government coercion to force the employer to supply the individual's device. It's wrong to make an employer buy you what you need if you're disabled, unless the company wants to do so. If it were not wrong, then the cost—however big or small—should not be an issue. If it's the company's unquestionable duty to buy someone a $100 amplifier then it's their duty to buy me a $10,000 leg. But in reality, the much greater cost of my leg over her amplifier shows that it's *not* the company's unquestionable duty. It's wrong for me to expect the company to make *me* whole when the company had nothing to do with my handicap. It was wrong for that woman to expect the same. It's our duty as employees and potential employees to make ourselves as able as possible for jobs that we want or else we should seek different jobs.

HIRE THE HANDICAPPED

The simple slogan, "Hire the Handicapped!" that was so common in a more normal, pre-1960s America worked. People actually did hire the handicapped. For one thing, handicapped employees often out-perform their peers. It may sound unlikely, but it's true. I'd hire in a heartbeat a handicapped person who wanted a job that her disability would allow her to do and who could demonstrate competence in that job. So would a lot of other employers before the ADA scared them from hiring so readily.

Once an individual has overcome a limitation, that individual has ample proof that he or she is an achiever. Think about people who impress you the most. They may be people who were born in a poor country who worked hard in America and developed, through their labors, something good. Perhaps it's someone who had a bad home life but still ended up successful at a sport. Perhaps it was someone who had handicaps, overcame them, and achieved success in a chosen field. Each of these cases shows individuals who not only inspire others but also have demonstrated that they can overcome obstacles. Chances are these people will continue to excel in whatever they want to do. If they want to work for me, I'd be a fool not to hire them.

If I were hiring a handicapped person who demonstrated success previously in overcoming that handicap without an attitude of entitlement, I'd want to hire that person. If that person needed something to do the job, such as a hearing amplifier, I would certainly consider getting it. I know that such an individual would probably be more reliable and show up for work more consistently, on the average, than others who did not have such a hurdle. So I'd weigh this employee's probable addition to my company with his request; if I felt that the cost justified my getting this employee over a competitor or some other company, I'd probably lean towards getting the device. But if I'm told by an employee that I have to buy something to make that person whole and he or she backs it up with the Americans with Disabilities Act, I immediately want to run from any future applicant who shows such problems. This is yet another way the Americans with Disabilities Act increases discrimination against the truly handicapped.

LEAVING EMPLOYERS IN THE DARK

Even though some people will fully disclose a disability during a job interview, if the disability is not obvious, many will not. Instead, they will get the job, show up for work, and then let the employer know about the problem. An employer must know about the handicap before the employer can do anything about it. Also, the employer needs to know before the hire what is expected. But the Americans with Disabilities Act encourages deception, either intentionally or unintentionally. The ADA's Title 1, section 102 (c)(2)(A) makes sure employers stay in the dark by stating, "[An employer] shall not conduct a medical examination or make inquiries of a job applicant as to whether such applicant is an individual with a disability or as to the nature or severity of such disability." While the ADA doesn't want the disabled, who are limited, to have limitations, it does not hesitate to place limitations on businesses that would otherwise not be limited. The ADA disables business and disables America in the name of removing disabilities.

Hudgins explains how this pre-hire limitation can hamstring a company:

An employer might easily determine the effect of a disability and screen out those not qualified for a job by giving an applicant a test–for example, asking a wheelchair-bound individual to place a heavy box on a top shelf in a warehouse, if that were one of the essential functions of the available job. But a more difficult problem is how to determine future costs that might only become apparent after an applicant is hired.

If he is not allowed to make inquires, how can an employer

know before the fact whether an employee will add an "undue hardship" or "substantial costs" to his business? And once an individual is hired, firing him because of a disability, no matter how costly that disability is to the business, virtually guarantees an ADA suit.[20]

Therefore, if you've got a problem that is not immediately obvious, the ADA enables you to hide that problem until you're hired. By then, it's too late to fire you if that problem incurs a high cost to your employer. Lew Rockwell, once again, clearly sees what the Americans with Disabilities Act has done to employers:

> A free market benefits employers and employees. Each person can find work that maximizes his contribution to the community of enterprise. And employers can find the right employee at the right price. The ADA abolished the market under the pretense of helping the handicapped, while actually insuring that they will be shunned as if they had a neon sign on their foreheads flashing, "Lawsuit, Lawsuit."[21]

THE TAX-BREAK BRIBE

In another slap to the handicapped, the government gives tax breaks to companies that provide jobs for the handicapped. If they just called these tax breaks "bribery" instead of "tax breaks," then too many people would realize they are nothing more than wrongful theft of the taxpayers' purse. The handicapped want to be hired because they have an ability to do the job they seek. They do not want to be hired so you can get a tax break. Yet disabled advocates certainly won't agree with me. The American Association of People with Disabilities (AAPD) recently stated that the government must increase communication regarding tax incentives so more companies will hire more disabled employees.[22] The idea communicated, however unintentional, is that employers should find value not in an employee's personal contribution to the company, but in the money they will save in taxes. To see how offensive this really is, compare the situation to a parent whose principal value in his children is the tax write-off.

Deb Cohen works for the Society for Human Resource Management as Vice President of Knowledge Development. Here is one piece of knowledge she must have developed herself: "With one in ten people estimated to have a severe disability, a large portion of the population is potentially being overlooked during the recruiting and hiring process."[23] She laments how few employers have taken advantage of incentives available to them when they hire *persons with disabilities*. She was responding to a Human Resource survey that revealed to ADA advocates what ADA opponents have known for years: Human Resource professionals believe that the ADA has created an increased fear of lawsuits.

One of AAPD's concerns is letting businesses know about the tax breaks they receive by remodeling for ADA compliance as well as for hiring disabled people. The tax breaks often only cover as much as 50 percent of such remodeling, but that other 50 percent is enough to put some small businesses out of business. In addition, I want an employer to hire me because I'm the best man for the job, not because he gets a tax break that his competitor won't get because I happened not to apply there. The disabled would not need to be used as pawns in these situations if the Americans with Disabilities Act had not sunk its teeth into the American dream in 1990.

EVERYBODY PAYS

When the advocates put their plans in place to create the ADA in 1990, their campaign of disabled person's victimhood was in full swing. They blamed employment troubles for the disabled on lack of accessibility and employer discrimination. Not only did the number of disabled employees decrease after the ADA's signing, even in the face of the booming 1990s, but federal disability payments increased sharply early in the ADA's history, going from $27 billion in 1991 to $37 billion in 1994.[24]

Common sense mandates that increasing the money available to unemployed disabled will lower the number of disabled who work. As usual, common sense proves to be correct.

Walter K. Olson describes how the American government focused on handicapped workers as far back as 1920 by implementing vocational rehabilitation programs (voc-rehab).[25] The intent was to put the handicapped to work. In doing this, the people behind voc-rehab made it their job to perform these tasks:

- Cajole employers to hire disabled workers

- Keep tabs on suitable job openings

- Consult on and sometimes pay for accommodations

- Train disabled people for jobs in their local markets

In other words, Olson clearly indicates that voc-rehab was doing what the ADA was later supposed to do. The voc-rehab program was in place seventy years before the ADA. Yet the ADA was still seen as necessary. Why?

For its first fifty years, until the 1970s, voc-rehab seemed to have success. At least, many disabled returning veterans and other disabled Americans were numbered successfully in the workplace. Whether voc-rehab had much to do with that employment is debatable, but the handicapped were working, and that was good.

The 1970s saw a tremendous drop in those workers. Although technological advances were being made that would give the handicapped even more leverage in the workplace, Olson describes how disabled employment was falling. In addition, the government started passing ADA-like laws and regulations for transportation and building codes, as well as making education changes that would encourage the handicapped. Still the employment numbers fell. Of course, these statistics were used by ADA advocates to get the ADA passed, but the reasons they cited for the declines were disingenuous at best due to what Olson calls the "Great Unmentionable": the Federal Social Security Disability Program.

As the Federal Social Security Disability Program expanded to include broader and more vague definitions of disability, the payments that program paid out went from $2.8 billion in 1970 to $24 billion in 1990! With such a tremendous increase in the paid-to-stay-home benefits, the government created a disincentive to work for the disabled and those claiming disabilities.[26] A few billion here and a few billion there and pretty soon we're talking about real money. The legal profession, instead of doctors, began diagnosing disabilities. The number of people who stayed at home and often made more from their payments than from working increased. You would certainly think that a decade and a half since the ADA's passing, such payments have decreased. Think again: *Inc. Magazine* estimates that 2003 saw about $71 billion in disability payments.[27]

In the face of unending costly ADA-related litigation, businesses are spending billions trying to settle complaints and get their businesses as compliant as they can. Meanwhile, the government spends billions competing against those businesses for the handicapped. The Federal Social Security Disability Program can ensure its existence only as long as it pays out funds to the disabled who accept their free money. Such funding directly obstructs free enterprise and hurts business for all Americans, those handicapped and those not.

6

Social Unrest and the ADA

I was guest-hosting a nationally syndicated television talk show that particular night. The show was tape-delayed, so the callers would not see their show until the following evening.

One caller told me that abortion was important in cases where the fetus was deformed. Remember, the show was tape-delayed and she had never seen me before.

As I reached up to scratch my nose twice, clearly showing my hands to the camera, I asked her, "For example if the fetus has deformed hands without even one normal finger?"

"Exactly!" was her reply.

I thanked her for the call and told her to tune in the next night to watch her call.[1]

The rather dull phrase "social issues" does not do justice to what are actually often life-and-death topics. Discussions of social issues such as this very book's primary topic—the government's approach to disabilities—are important so that people will understand the costs that are at stake. When quality of life is changed due to governmental policy, people need to understand that change so they can work to embrace it or abolish it. *Disabling America* has worked to show you that the Americans with Disabilities Act erodes America legally, financially, and socially. You need to be aware of that decay and the cost and damage it causes for you, your family, and our nation. When your standard of living is threatened, even a little bit at a time as it is daily with the ADA's direct and indirect costs, you should know about it.

OFFENSE IS RELATIVE

Children grow up singing the taunting phrase, "Sticks and stones can break my bones but words will never hurt me." Don't believe it, and don't teach that to your children. If your children happen to use certain words and phrases around an ADA lawyer, the words they speak could very well hurt them. Those who dare speak out against the ADA and its ilk are likely to be accused of a hate crime. The ADA has its own definition of hate speech. Mock the disabled and you could go to jail. Admit it, after all you've now read, the fact that merely talking about the disabled might be termed a hate crime is not a big surprise to you, right? The Department of Justice takes the ADA seriously; after all, the jobs there are at stake.

The Federal Bureau of Investigation even collects statistics related to what they call "hate crimes" against the disabled. This book might require that they get new calculators. In tracking hate crimes against the disabled, they segregate and profile the disabled. The mere act of collecting such data further shows the handicapped that they are different from normal people in society. The state of Idaho, among others, singles out such people even further by tracking the number of "Anti-Physically Disabled" hate crimes and "Anti-Mentally Disabled" hate crimes that occur in any given year.[2]

Business owners and employers know best whom to hire. Only they can determine the most skilled for any given position. The government is, by its very nature, the least skilled organization in matching resources to a best-needs fit. The most inferior ADA rules have now supplanted the job of the most superior business owner.

Consider virtually any government position that you deal with in everyday life that is not directly part of a local or national protection or rescue organization (jobs that only a government can do properly and with authority). Be honest: was the best applicant the one chosen for that government position? Every once in a while the best applicant might be hired; just as every once in a while a private business will hire a loser. Consider though the general government worker's attitude and the rules you must follow while interacting with that employee, such as at the department of motor vehicles. Now judge the ability of the state to properly utilize resources and people. The blame for common failure of such positions falls on the government's unwillingness and inability to be accountable in any way.

The same kinds of inefficient, uncaring, faceless government officials are now the ones telling you who is best for your job openings. They decide how much money you as a taxpayer must spend when they take a business owner to court. They decide how much money you as a taxpayer must spend to pay the business owner's damages through a higher cost of living. You pay both sides in all ADA battles. You cannot win. Those officials in authority are the ones who want to put you in jail if you speak out against the disabled. And they are the ones who want to determine whether you have spoken out or not. They set the rules, they set the penalties, and they haul you to court. They are just following regulations: regulations they designed.

Lew Rockwell believes the ADA has damaged America's business hiring decisions. He has said, "The ADA has delivered blow after blow to liberty. It has forced employers to hire and promote according to the government's priorities and not those of the enterprise."[3]

According Justin Dart Jr., who has polio and is the former chairman of the President's Committee on Employment of People with Disabilities, the world often hates the handicapped so hate crimes are on the rise. "Today in America," says Dart, "there's a frightening backlash against not only disabled people, but minorities, women, gays, and all those whose civil rights need protection."[4] No doubt, this statement would make most truly handicapped people feel extremely uncomfortable. It also echoes the description of what ADA advocates had to do to get the ADA passed. That is, victims must be made out of non-victims and the sooner the better.

Certainly, throughout the ages, handicapped people have had problems from jerks they happen to run into. But so have non-handicapped people. Anecdotal evidence of such incidents, which common sense tells you are few and far between, does not make a good case that the disabled are viewed negatively in American society. In my extensive world travels, I don't see discrimination against the handicapped in great numbers—or small numbers—anywhere on earth. In fact, I see quite the opposite. People who don't know me often spend far too much attention trying to help me when I do not need or desire help with whatever I'm doing.

My conclusion is that the handicapped *are* victims. They are victims of the Americans with Disabilities Act and victims of the people behind that law who planned it, wrote it, promote it, and litigate in its name.

Kathi Wolfe quotes Marca Bristo, chair of the National Council on Disability, in her article for the leftist magazine *The Progressive*, "Bashing the Disabled: The New Hate Crime": "We shouldn't be surprised by the backlash. It happens in our society whenever a constituency fights for its civil rights."[5] (Does absolutely nobody question these ridiculous headlines and article assumptions these days?)

Chapter Four plainly shows that the details surrounding the ADA's origin severely question the need for the ADA. Handicapped people were viewed with high esteem in society at the time, and it took ADA advocates a lot of strategy to turn that esteem into victimhood.

Wolfe goes on to quote Dart:

> One manifestation of this backlash is hate crimes against the disabled.
>
> We've become a scapegoat. Some people who don't wish to hear about our country's economic or social problems—who want to ignore civil-rights issues—blame disabled people for these problems. Sometimes that gets acted out in hateful rhetoric or hate crimes.

To bolster his case, Dart notes that disability activists actually "made the list of groups that the Unabomber says he disapproves of."[6]

I agree that the left-wing eco-murderer called the Unabomber probably doesn't like the handicapped. Nevertheless, society as a whole doesn't share that dislike. I would wager that absolutely nobody blames disabled people for the country's economic and social problems. My word opposes Dart's word on that, and he's known as the "Father of the Americans with Disabilities Act."[7] Seriously though, can anyone really flag a single Matthew Shepard or James Byrd-style murder of the handicapped, let alone slews of them? The reason that hate crime legislation has expanded is not due to the needs of the disabled but due to the needs of those who advocate for the ADA. Senator Bob Dole is the one who worked to change the Hate Crimes Statistics Act to include disabled. (Countless conservatives are still scratching their heads over why they cast a vote for him in the 1996 presidential election.)

CAREFUL WITH THE FRUITCAKE

The *Boston Globe* recently described how Bruce Bruneau of the Massachusetts Office on Disabilities was disciplined and forced to apologize when a colleague with a brain injury filed a complaint.[8] Bruneau used the term "fruitcake" in public, a term he used to refer to a business owner who refused to address handicapped access concerns. That's just nutty. The complaint was filed by Robert Edwards, a man who has brain injuries, who also works for a Massachusetts disability commission, or he did, before he resigned over this matter. He no longer holds his position on that Framingham Disability Commission because of his opinion that fruitcake is a derogatory term used to describe people with brain injuries. Debra Kamen, director of the Statewide Head Injury Program, also weighed in on the matter. She said that she had never heard of the term "fruitcake" being used to describe those with brain-injuries. Given her job, she should know. Nevertheless, Debra Kamen did comment further on the matter. It's her hope that Bruneau is merely "ignorant and just needs to be educated."[9]

Quite a bit of energy was spent on the fruitcake remark. Keep in mind that "fruitcake" referred to someone who was not following proper ADA accommodation requests. It's almost as though hate speech trumps actual ADA violations.

THE LANGUAGE POLICE

Diane Ravitch's book, *The Language Police*, describes the censorship of books and the censorship of test topics for government school students.[10] Hate speech is axed the moment censors such as ADA advocates decree it. For example, a passage that describes peanuts was banned due to some students' allergies to the nuts. The use and nutritional knowledge about peanuts was deemed less important than the self-esteem of those few allergic students.

Even more bizarre was Ravitch's description of the "heroic blind youth" who climbed to the top of Mt. McKinley. Remember that ADA advocates don't want handicapped accomplishments praised. Such praise keeps others from viewing the handicapped as victims. Ravitch goes on to describe why the blind youth's ascent to the top of Mt. McKinley would never make its way into the government school textbooks:

Stranger still, a story about a heroic blind youth who climbed to the top of Mt. McKinley was rejected [by the textbook panel], not only because of its implicit suggestion that blind people might have a harder time than people with sight, but also because it was alleged to contain "regional bias": According to the panel's bizarre way of thinking, students who lived in non-mountainous areas would theoretically be at a "disadvantage" in comprehending a story about mountain climbing.

Stories set in deserts, cold climates, tropical climates, or by the seaside, Ravitch learned, are similarly *verboten* as test topics, since not all students have had personal experience of these regions.[11]

The self-esteem and praise for what this youth accomplished is completely unimportant to the advocates.

ONTARIO SHOCKER

This statement from an *Ottawa Citizen* article speaks for itself:

The province of Ontario is developing guidelines which will formally spell out how workers in state-run homes may assist the disabled to have sex. The province is wading into this uncharted territory after six health care workers at a home for the disabled in Barrie, Ontario, complained that they were fired for refusing to accept a new policy they say asked them to masturbate their clients.[12]

Certainly, Ontario is not covered under the Americans with Disabilities Act. Nevertheless, if you do not foresee the ADA as eventually requiring this here in America, you may need to reread this book's previous chapters.

Such "work" should not be tolerated, let alone required. Government workers are the last group of people who should be allowed to interact in a patient's sex life. Yet when the state becomes the saving factor to a people, the state begins to take over areas that family members would be disallowed from doing. If a family member, for example, did what these state-paid workers were asked to do, the family member would be jailed for sex crimes—and rightly so. Yet, when a government worker puts himself in the middle of a sex act, it's known as a compassionate act.

HOMOSEXUALS AND OTHERS JOIN THE ACT

I went on national television a few years ago and stated that the homosexual leaders would begin to use the Americans with Disabilities Act to further many of their causes. I was mocked for saying that. U.S. Senator Jesse Helms worked to ensure that the Americans with Disabilities Act would not protect discrimination against transvestites and transsexuals. Helms has since retired; the ADA has not. If anything, it shows signs of picking up steam. Recent rulings have allowed transsexuals under the big and growing disabled tent. Many AIDS-related ADA cases are also on the books. The homosexual agenda is now using the ADA, as are so many other groups, to promote their own desires. I've always stated that the ADA seemed perfectly timed to help homosexual causes. I believe that the ADA's timing in 1990 fit the needs of the homosexual agenda and its public outcries around that time calling for an end to discrimination and promoting themselves as society's latest downtrodden victims.

Students at the University of California in San Diego (UCSD) are petitioning the college to create unisex bathrooms. To make this happen, the Associated Students of UCSD unanimously passed a resolution that, in their words, will make their campus a "more welcoming place to everyone."[13] The reason for the conversion to unisex bathrooms may not be obvious to the general *Disabling America* reader. At first you might suspect that the eighteen– to twenty-two-year-old students just want to enjoy the perceived benefits of sharing bathrooms with the opposite sex. But it seems that these students are far too altruistic to want the bathrooms changed for their own personal, selfish desires. How could their reason for the unisex bathrooms be degenerate when they clearly state that all they want is to *"make transsexuals more comfortable."* To quote student advocate Brie Finegold, this resolution helps create a campus that is a safe and "inclusive space for everyone, specifically parents, students with disabilities, and students whose sex is not readily apparent." So if you're a parent of a UCSD student, you perhaps now feel better knowing that those tuition dollars allow you to go to the bathroom with the boys, girls, and transsexuals—all at the same time. How relieving.

OFFICIALLY PROTECTING TRANSSEXUALS

Carlos Enriquez was a doctor from Camden County. He was a member of the College of New Jersey's trustee board.[14] In 1997, the West Jersey Health System fired Enriquez when he began wearing earrings, letting his hair grow long, grew breasts, and polished his fingernails. He then changed his name to Carla and had operations that changed his anatomy to look like that of a woman's.

It's interesting to note that most news stories covering this do not mention right away that Enriquez is a pediatrician; they bury that vital information in the center or towards the end of their reports. If the reader were to be given that knowledge early in the story, that reader would be even more likely to see Enriquez's lawsuit as a miscarriage of justice.

At first, a lower court refused to rule in favor of Enriquez. After shopping for a better judge, Enriquez and his counsel found the New Jersey state appeals court. The court ruled that discrimination against transsexuals is not allowed under state law and that transsexualism can be considered a disability. The court wrote the following:

> It is incomprehensible to us that our Legislature would ban discrimination against heterosexual men and women; against homosexual men and women . . . but would condone discrimination against men or women who seek to change their anatomical sex because they suffer from a gender identity disorder.

A person who is discriminated against because he changes his gender from male to female is being discriminated against because he or she is a member of a very small minority whose condition remains incomprehensible to most individuals. . . . Past opinions are too constricted.[15]

According to journalist Nick Manetto, the court actually ruled that transexualism is a handicap. Manetto attempted to contact Enriquez for a comment, but the reporter could not locate him (her?).

Arthur Jarrett, Enriquez's attorney, was described as being ecstatic over the decision. It should be noted for the record that most attorneys are ecstatic when they win a case. The more transsexuals want to be considered as normal, the happier they are to be considered disabled and abnormal it appears to me. It's difficult to keep up with their needs (assuming you have the desire to try).

AUTOIMMUNE *DISABLING* SYNDROME

In early 1998, the Clinton Justice Department, headed by Attorney General Janet Reno, urged the Supreme Court to rule that people infected with AIDS should be protected by the Americans with Disabilities Act. The case involved an AIDS-infected woman who claimed disability because she was substantially limited in the "major life activity" of reproduction because an HIV-positive pregnant woman risks transmitting the virus to her child.[16] But she went on to plead that the HIV infection *even without symptoms* constituted a disability automatically.

The United States Justice Department helped bring AIDS into the ADA-protected class by asserting that the department had long considered HIV to be a disability "because the reactions of others to infected individuals cause such individuals to be treated as though they were disabled." In other words, if someone reacts to you as though you have a deadly, contagious disease and you do have a deadly, contagious disease, then you're disabled and those people are just uncaring bigots.

♿

HIS SEX MADE HIM DO IT

An Illinois Department of Public Aid caseworker named Richard N. Shick sued the department where he worked. He claimed that he was discriminated against because of his disabilities and "his sex" (thankfully, no details are provided about what he meant by "his sex").[17]

The traumas of his disabilities and his sex apparently caused him to rob a Joliet, Illinois, convenience store with a sawed-off shotgun. His jury awarded him $5 million in damages plus $166,700 in back pay due to his disability that forced him into this life of crime.

The United States District Court for the Southern District of Illinois dismissed the judgment. Nevertheless, as is so often the case, Shick still hit the ADA jackpot because while still in prison, the District Court went ahead and awarded him $303,830 in front pay (pay he would miss the ten years he would be in jail). Let's hope that he can get rehabilitated from his disabilities and from his sex while in prison.

ADA'S UNTOUCHABLES

Let me offer unequivocal proof that the people behind the ADA and those who advocate strengthening the ADA are disingenuous and generally could not care less about those who are truly disabled. I warn you, this glaring inconsistency will quell all doubts, so if you still want to believe that the Americans with Disabilities Act and its advocates genuinely care about the truly handicapped then you may want to skip this section. I'd not want to be one to let truth, facts, and proof stand in the way of what you insist on believing. If the topic were not so serious, I would not feel the need to be so blunt.

One room exists where no ADA advocate, attorney, or Department of Justice official would *ever* enter to stop an ADA violation. That room is any abortionist's office where a baby is being aborted if the reason used is spina bifida. This holds true not just for spina bifida but for any reason given where the mother is convinced that her baby won't have a chance at a normal life.

Abortion is often suggested for unborn babies diagnosed with Down's syndrome and physical deformities. spina bifida, Down's syndrome, and physical handicaps are never seen as disabilities that warrant accommodation when it's an unborn baby who has any of these problems inside the womb. Therefore, if an unborn little girl with such problems is about to be violently removed from her mother's womb—a place that should be her safest haven on earth, ADA advocates turn a blind eye and tackle more needy victims. Such victims might include ones like the motorist who got a ticket for not wearing a seat belt and didn't want to pay it, so he turned around and sued Topeka, Kansas, for giving him the ticket; his ADA defense was claustrophobia.[18] Now *he* was certainly well-represented by the ADA.

The ADA wants your babies to have perfect, designer genes—or else. This is actually short-sighted of them. From a selfish perspective, one would think that ADA advocates would prefer as many handicapped babies born as possible. The more babies born with disabilities the more justified the ADA would see itself. The only completely unprotected class of people left on earth is the innocent group inside their mothers' wombs. The Spina Bifida Association of America gives the details of the condition:

> Neural tube defects (NTDs) are serious birth defects that involve incomplete development of the brain, spinal cord and/or protective coverings for these organs.
>
> Most infants born with anencephaly do not survive more than a few hours after birth. Encephalocele results in a hole in the skull through which brain tissue protrudes. Although most babies with encephalocele do not live or are severely retarded, early surgery has been able to save a few children.[19]

Such operations will only improve their success rate as technology and knowledge about such diseases continue to increase. The fact that surgery has been able to save some children and the fact that children have been diagnosed with spina bifida in the womb and been born to live many years does not and will not matter in these hands-off, no-questions-asked abortionists' offices. No ADA official will be there to take them into custody for violating the disabled baby's rights. Think about it: an ADA advocate will jump at the chance to defend against the violation of a gambler's right to his addiction, but that same advocate would never dream of protecting the most important, genuine, and precious right of all: the right to life.

NOT FULLY HUMAN

ADA advocates are fast to point out that the disabled are "fully human." That phrase is bandied about as if it were their motto. In my view their blind eye towards the slaughter of unborn handicapped babies seems to violate their self-proclaimed "fully human" manifesto for the disabled. Otherwise, the advocates would be in every abortionist's building and OB/GYN clinic to ensure that the handicapped are protected and that they remain "fully human" as opposed to dead humans.

My personal observation is that many who support the Americans with Disabilities Act—not the Americans who know little about it who assume it's an okay thing but those who developed it and who promote it and who make livings suing others because of it—these people often seem to me to connect with the crowds who are pro-choice. As long as the baby doesn't have a choice to live—the pro-choice crowd seems extremely happy. Obviously, not all ADA advocates will fall into the abortion-for-the-handicapped crowd, but as I said, it's my personal observation that their ideologies and world views seem to correlate well with the people who support abortion-on-demand of the handicapped.

THE ORIGIN OF THE END

Margaret Sanger founded Planned Parenthood. Planned Parenthood is America's largest abortion provider. Planned Parenthood still gives awards in Sanger's honor, such as when Planned Parenthood gave its Margaret Sanger Award to the BBC for its documentary called "The Dying Rooms."[20]

The documentary described events in China that surround China's one-child policy. In China, it is against the law to have a baby sister or a baby brother. Families that do conceive a second child are required to abort that second child. "The Dying Rooms" undercover camera crew exposed the horrors behind the mistreatment and subsequent murders of little siblings. This occurs in China's state-run orphanages, which brings new meaning to the term "orphanage" of which I was formerly unfamiliar. Planned Parenthood approves of China's pro-choice policy where every second child *must* be killed. One must ask where the choice is in this pro-choice policy.

On a vacation to China, I asked our Chinese tour guide about China's one-child policy. He lamented that he and his wife wanted a little girl but they already had a boy. He did perk up right away and say that China has a wonderful policy where each man, woman, and child (he didn't need to say "only child") had to plant one tree every year. Nationally, therefore, this country is proud that each family plants three new trees each year and kills all second babies. I've never heard of a single person who earns an income from the Americans with Disabilities Act ever petitioning the American government to speak out against this tragedy.

The very week we were in Beijing, in 1995, the World Health Organization was there celebrating the United Nation's Women's Conference. With a straight face, Hillary Rodham Clinton made a speech that included these words:

> By gathering in Beijing, we are focusing world attention on issues that matter most in the lives of women and their families: access to

education, health care, jobs, and credit, the chance to enjoy basic legal and human rights and participate fully in the political life of their countries.[21]

Planned Parenthood's Web site further encouraged China when it stated:

With the largest gathering ever to attend a United Nations conference, the Fourth World Conference on Women is held in Beijing, China, and produces a Platform for Action that reaffirms women's rights as human rights, calls for the decriminalization of women who undergo abortions in countries where it is illegal . . . .[22]

In other words, Planned Parenthood doesn't want the abortions to stop, only the law against abortions changed. In China, it's a legal requirement to murder your baby sister, and Planned Parenthood holds such a model up to the rest of the world to follow.

Given founder Margaret Sanger's own writings, Planned Parenthood was not honoring the "The Dying Rooms" film's exposure of the murders as much as they were honoring the murders themselves. Margaret Sanger scorned what she called the "Asiatic races," and she wanted their numbers to be drastically reduced.[23]

To further the probability that Planned Parenthood gave the Margaret Sanger Award to the BBC documentary in support of its subject as opposed to agreeing that the exposed orphanage murders were doing wrong, you should consider the very first Margaret Sanger Award (which they sometimes lightheartedly call the *Maggie Award*) given to Martin Luther King. Sanger had what she called her "Negro project" intended to dramatically decrease the number of blacks. Today, the African-American population has been reduced by as much as one-third due to abortion, most of which took place inside Planned Parenthood buildings. Today, two black babies are aborted for every three that make it out alive.[24] Therefore, Margaret Sanger's dream is being fulfilled long after her death. Sanger, before her death, had wanted to give an award to Dr. King in order to use him. She made it clear that such an award was to be given only after explaining that, "We do not want word to go out that we want to exterminate the Negro population and the Minister [Dr. King] is the man who can straighten out that idea if it ever occurs to any of their more rebellious members."[25]

It turns out that blacks had cause for worry. "The mass of Negroes," Planned Parenthood's founder Sanger once said, "particularly in the South, still breed carelessly and disastrously, with the result that the increase among Negroes, even more than among whites, is from the portion of the population least intelligent and fit, and least able to rear children properly."[26]

So Sanger wanted her organization to use Dr. King in the hopes that he would cover up the fact that they performed a targeted slaughter of the black race, if such information were ever exposed to the public.

ABORTION TARGETS THE HANDICAPPED

Although the previous text was not directly related to handicapped issues, that background is vital for you to know if you care about handicapped children growing up to become happy, healthy citizens. Now that you understand the background of Planned Parenthood, you might better accept the fact that a major Planned Parenthood target was, and is, the handicapped. Claiming that unborn children with handicaps don't have a decent chance at normal life, Planned Parenthood supports the murder of unborn handicapped children—and the ADA could not be more willfully blind to that fact.

As Steven W. Mosher wrote in the *Wall Street Journal*, Sanger's hatred of children went far beyond race:

> In her 1922 book "Pivot of Civilization" she unabashedly called for the extirpation of "weeds . . . overrunning the human garden"; for the segregation of "morons, misfits, and the maladjusted"; and for the sterilization of "genetically inferior races." It was later that she singled out the Chinese, writing in her autobiography about

"the incessant fertility of [the Chinese] millions spread like a plague."

There can be no doubt that Sanger would have been wildly enthusiastic over China's one-child policy, for her "Code to Stop Overproduction of Children," published in 1934, decreed that "no woman shall have a legal right to bear a child without a permit . . . no permit shall be valid for more than one child." As for China's selective elimination of handicapped and abandoned babies, she would have been delighted that Beijing had heeded her decades-long call for exactly such eugenicist policies.[27]

Those eugenicist policies that Sanger wrote about in detail are not just coming true in Beijing. Planned Parenthood and other abortionists all over America feel no hesitation to use a birth defect as an excuse to get rid of a baby. The Americans with Disabilities Act's original (and false) figure of 43 million disabled Americans never was to include disabled babies still in their mom's womb—these, the ADA advocates completely and willfully ignore. Although ADA activists are certainly going to challenge this chapter's assumptions, the proof is in the pudding.

♿

A SIMPLE TEST

One popular Web site offers this test:

QUESTION: A woman has tuberculosis and the father has syphilis. Together they have had four children. The first child was born blind. The second child was stillborn. The third child was deaf and dumb. Their fourth child was born with tuberculosis. The woman is now pregnant with their fifth child. Would you recommend abortion?

ANSWER: If so, you would have killed Ludwig van Beethoven.[28]

INCREASING BIRTH DEFECTS

The number of birth defects has risen over the past several decades. The cause for many of these defects is simply unknown. Sometimes, a birth defect is traceable to a cause, such as might happen when an alcoholic or drug-addicted mother's actions hurt the baby.

One current birth-related concern is the increase in premature birth rates. Prematurity can lead to major disabilities or even death for the prematurely born baby. Fortunately, research shows some answers that help develop premature babies more successfully so that their lives can be normal. The March of Dime's medical director, Dr. Nancy Green, recently told *Time* magazine that premature deliveries have risen 27 percent in the past few years She states that the cause for these premature babies "is a mystery."[29]

Dr. Green needs to check the medical literature once again. Dr. David C. Reardon who directs the Elliott Institute that researches post-abortion results writes that at least 48 published studies have shown a significantly higher risk of premature birth and low-birth-weight deliveries among women who have had abortions. He points out that

> One of the best studies found the risk [for premature birth] doubled after just one abortion. Multiple abortions increase the risk even more. A doubling of risk among an estimated one-fourth of delivering women who have a prior history of abortion would result in a 25 percent rise overall.[30]

The March of Dimes is an organization that publicly dedicates itself to preventing birth defects and premature babies. Dr. Reardon implies that the March of Dimes' money-generating machine is more important than their results [of decreasing birth defects]. I must say that my findings from studying their Web site make me tend to agree with his assessment.

On the March of Dimes Web site the first words you see are: "March of Dimes, Saving babies, together.[31] Support the March of Dimes by Donating Now!" Donations are certainly high on their priority list as few charities would put an exclamation mark after *Donate Now!* Of course, if the March of Dimes gets most of its funding from donations, they should be able to get those donations any way they think is best as long as they are not disingenuous. At the time of this writing, directly under the exclamatory plea for donations, the March of Dimes Web site has a large section called *National Campaign: Prematurity* that states (relating to premature births), "The answers can't come soon enough." They state that one of every eight babies in the United States is born prematurely. They say that some are so tiny they can't even cry. Then another plea: "If they could [cry], it would be for your help."

How can you help? By giving to the March of Dimes. *Donate Now!* I assure you that if giving to the March of Dimes truly helps, that is what you should do. But read the rest of this section before writing that check just so you know the complete story.

After exploring the March of Dimes' Web site, I read this statement about the cause of prematurity that creates so many babies with problems:

> While doctors have made tremendous advances in caring for babies born too small and too soon, we need to find out how to prevent these tragedies from happening in the first place. Despite decades of research, scientists have not yet developed effective ways to help prevent premature delivery.

Again, that simply is not true. Abortion contributes greatly to prematurity. Why haven't Americans with Disabilities Act advocates contacted the March of Dimes to let them know how to lower the number of premature births? A simple call for a campaign to stop abortion would help end *two* tragedies: handicapped babies murdered by abortionists and subsequent babies who suffer handicaps or die due to prematurity-related causes.

Disabling America is not a book about the March of Dimes, obviously, but primarily about the ADA and how the ADA has harmed the handicapped. I must say that I can find no place where the Americans with Disabilities Act advocates are trying to work with the March of Dimes, or anywhere on their own, to help prevent the disabilities brought about by premature births by making the public aware of abortion's dangers.

As long as the March of Dimes and other kinds of major organizations in America remain silent on abortion and its negative after-effects to the mother and to subsequent babies, the Americans with Disabilities Act will have clients.

THE ADA SMELLS

Moving from such a weighty topic, we turn to one light as air—in fact the very odor wafting off your body. If you smell *bad*, you cannot be discriminated against under the Americans with Disabilities Act. Yes, the ADA protects your right to stink. Curiously, if you smell *good*, you can be considered offensive under the Americans with Disabilities Act. The ADA will litigate if you insist on smelling good.

The more one learns about the ADA's short history, the more one stops being surprised at its absurdities. *Reader's Digest* studied Justice Department and EEOC complaints. Discrimination was claimed for the following situations: Body odor, myopia, morning sickness, chronic fatigue syndrome, infertility, obesity, multiple chemical sensitivity, attention-deficit disorder, and anxiety brought about by a supervisor's reprimand.[32] Body odor, it is maintained, should not be a factor, for example, in your employment. If you want to work in customer service or you want to lead hospital tours or want to work as a perfume salesperson at Macy's, your body odor cannot be a consideration in your employment. If it becomes a consideration, the ADA will step in to take that problem away, and your employer will be made to pay dearly.

To learn that the ADA takes offense when you smell good, you need only to look at Shutesbury, Massachusetts, which has created "fragrance zones" for their town meetings. It seems that some people cannot tolerate the smell of cologne, perfumes, or deodorant.[33] When the meetings begin, people are segregated by scent. Those who don't use deodorant will sit in one area while those who do will sit in another. I would predict that those who do use deodorant appreciate all this. Of course, this isn't so the good-smelling people don't have to sit with the others, it's so the others don't have to sit with the good-smelling ones. David Ames is a Shutesbury Town Administrator who is proud of making his town compliant with the ADA. He says that using fragrances is like smoking in public.

THE COURT GETS ONE RIGHT

A needle in a haystack is what I call an ADA case that is properly thrown out of the courts. In the overwhelming number of cases, the plaintiff wins either in a settlement or in the court. The defendant always loses given the amount of money that must be spent on the defense. The attorneys for both sides generally always get paid. Nevertheless, you can actually find a story here and there where the plaintiff gets nothing. These cases really stand out in this world of ADA litigation. For some reason, the tossing out is almost always done by a higher court.

Charlotte Davis attempted to convince an Alabama federal judge that her acute hemorrhoid condition constituted ADA protection.[34] Davis worked as a store manager for BellSouth Mobility at the time of her request. The judge ruled, "To characterize such a common malady as hemorrhoids, even severe hemorrhoids, as a disability would thwart the purposes of the ADA."

When you look at the origins of the Americans with Disabilities Act as well as the draconian activities done in its name ever since, this case's result is a pleasant surprise.

7

CHILDREN AND DISABLED EDUCATION

"You should have seen it," my former high school English teacher told my mother. "I had not been back there in years. But as I walked to the front, I saw they were wheeling bedridden children through the door. These children could not even speak or function outside these hospital beds without care. They were taking them into the same classes as the regular students!"

She continued, "This is due to their experiment called mainstreaming. *How can anybody learn in that atmosphere?"*[1]

T hose in charge of education today don't seem to put learning high on their priority list. Experiments in science class have been replaced by experiments in social engineering. Chaos abounds when schools mainstream handicapped students into regular classes. Education and chaos are mutually exclusive—education cannot and will not take place in such environments.

The concept of "mainstreaming" involves putting severely handicapped students in the same classes as regular students along with other students labeled as "disabled." Teachers and administrators supposedly do this so the disabled children's self-esteem will improve. The thought is that the handicapped will not view themselves as being different. They have added special school diapering rooms for students who are not toilet trained, as is sometimes the case with severe Down's syndrome, mental retardation, autism, brain injuries, and physical disabilities. Fortunately they have not mainstreamed these students in regular bathrooms and put diapering stations there. Yet these special education students who need diapering cause a great concern when one considers how many able-bodied children are molested in the government schools. It must cause the parents of these poor students overwhelming concerns when they read about another molestation in a school because their children who need help with toileting are at much greater risk by their situations.

The sad truth is that teachers will, on the altar of these kids' mental and physical health, say they are improving those poor precious children's self-esteem. When you grow up and your teachers and schools tell you that you cannot make it without being labeled special, you are assured of having low self-esteem.

The teachers and administrators then feel good about doing something. The results are less important than the process. Handicapped and regular students in the public schools today are often used as pawns in such mainstreaming programs. Handicapped students in the classroom bring in big bucks.

A VERY BAD IDEA

IDEA is an acronym for the Individuals with Disabilities Education Act. The act, sometimes called Public Law 94-142, was first approved in 1975 and has been strengthened and reauthorized since. Looking at IDEA's results since 1975, one would think the program would simply be cancelled. Instead, it gets more money and more support each year (something that frequently happens with failed government programs), along with cries of "reform" that often come from the very people who abuse IDEA and who would never allow true reform. A bad IDEA should not be reformed, a bad IDEA should be eliminated. Instead of either, though, it keeps growing by billions of dollars.

IDEA and the ADA go hand in hand. ADA contains no specific education rules or requirements in its purest form because IDEA already existed. Without IDEA, the ADA surely would have included IDEA's concepts. School facilities are covered under Title II of the ADA's public entities clause, so they have been modified to conform to ADA building requirements. This book's Appendix contains text from Title II.

As of September 2002, IDEA had become a $50 billion-a-year program. Under IDEA's umbrella, each public school must create an individualized education program for each disabled student. After developing a student's individual education program, the school invites students' parents for a long series of meetings where the program is presented. Although it appears that the parental input is needed, parents soon find out how little input they have. This process typically creates a wider and wider chasm between the teacher and parent until the parent feels threatened and marginalized. According to Robert Holland who writes for the *School Reform News*, the parents deeply familiar with bureaucracy and the law (pardon my redundancy) will fare better than those who do not know how such systems operate. Holland says the "professional jargon and procedural hardball" that the schools play against the parents intimidate them until they either back away from involvement (the school's preference) or sue the school.[2]

The special education teachers generally get paid more than the other teachers at schools. They have smaller class sizes. This has resulted in friction between these teachers and the rest. Politics are always a major issue in a government job, and the special education program has only added to that conflict. Such discord further erodes the children's education.

The bed-ridden and other truly handicapped students comprise a very small amount of the disabled student population. Yet their requirements are massive and put tremendous strain on other students who are there to learn. Many others are labeled "learning disabled." This category has grown so large that now eight out of ten learning disabled students are labeled as such because they cannot read.[3] Before the 1960s, the fault for this absence of reading skills would have been placed on the institution. Now, the burden is placed on the victim: the child.

As a side note, it is interesting to see that as phonics was removed from the government schools to teach reading, reading abilities dramatically plummeted. The *whole language* approach used by so many schools today almost guarantees failure at reading. If eight in ten learning disabled students are labeled as such because they cannot read, one should find it interesting that such a direct correlation exists between the use of the whole language approach and the number of learning disabled students. The more whole language is used, the more learning disabled students exist. By removing the phonic method of reading, the schools have assured themselves of more and more disabled customers.

In other words, the schools create their customer base by creating students who cannot read and are then able to be stuck in special education programs. Cigarette makers are blamed because their ads are sometimes aimed at children, virtually ensuring the companies' income in the future. Yet, the major news outlets never discuss the government school practice of using children to generate future special education income-producing customers.

Dr. Arthur B. Robinson of the Oregon Institute of Science and Medicine says it best: "Public schooling in California and in most other locations has become little more than a tax-financed, institutionalized form of child abuse."[4]

Given that the more of these illiterate children labeled as "special" exist, the more funding the school system gets. The number of special education students rose 242 percent between 1979 and 1997. In Baltimore, only one percent of the 2001 class of special education eighth graders scored satisfactory or better on the Maryland performance examinations.[5] Maryland is an anomaly because, as you'll see later in this chapter, special education students usually are not allowed anywhere near standardized tests. Once labeled as a special education student early in their education, such children are marked for life. Given that, it's so strange to read now one of IDEA's goals: To provide the special programs designed to educate and create opportunities for disabled students.

A total of more than $77 billion is now used annually for K-12 education of special education students. (That is a *b* in *billion*—we're not talking about paltry millions when we discuss our cost of the worst government educational system in the developed world.) Twenty-one percent of the overall total education budget is spent on these students. The budget is designed to further the special education process and IDEA's adherence. Funding is in no way related to a child's educational improvement. Therefore, much more effort is placed on the process of following the rules to get the money than teaching the students.

Robert Holland verifies this true IDEA/special education goal when he writes:

The Individuals with Disabilities in Education Act (IDEA) has dissolved into a litigious morass that values process more highly than each child's achieving good results. . . . Because IDEA funding is based on regulatory compliance rather than producing academic results, perhaps it is unsurprising that states focus on bureaucratic process instead of academic improvement.[6]

DISABLED STUDENTS DISABLE OTHERS

If the student focus is not education, as the results seem to imply, then what does a special education student get out of the deal? Impunity.

Changes to IDEA are often talked about. A bill called HR 1350 seeks to reduce slightly the burden of IDEA and extends IDEA to transfer to a voucher program for private schools. This will help harm private schools in the same way IDEA harms the government schools. Most disability groups and teacher organizations oppose HR 1350 and just about any other recommendation to correct IDEA's stronghold.

In one surprising move, however, an actual true overhaul of part of IDEA has been requested by the National Education Association–not because of any harm to students but to that of a teacher. A disabled student attending under the IDEA plan at a North Carolina school broke his teacher's arm. A disabled Oklahoma student stabbed her teacher with a nail.[7] Such stories should make you wonder how they can apply the term "disabled" to such students. The punishment for these criminals was that they would not be called criminals. Each received suspension from school for less than a week.

The NEA and the American Federation of Teachers have both demanded an overhaul of IDEA so that violent and disruptive classroom behavior by those labeled as disabled does not continue. Such incidents are far too common, ranging from "defecating in the classroom to the regular battering of teachers and even murder of other students."[8]

At least one group is working to silence this talk about IDEA's reform. The Disability Rights Education and Defense Fund opposes any change to IDEA in any way unless that change is to strengthen its stranglehold and income. This group headquarters in Berkeley, California. In 1997, IDEA was amended slightly with Public Law 105-17 (also called IDEA '97). IDEA '97 indicated that disabled students would participate in state and district-wide testing but does not specify that the tests taken will be the same as those the non-disabled students take. Schools can now discipline disabled students with up to ten days of suspension. The NEA and its peers' fear of guns allowed them to increase that suspension to forty-five days if a gun was involved in a school crime. That will show those kids how to behave! (I would have loved suspension! I'm old enough to remember getting spanked in school so I usually behaved. A promise of suspension would have made my day!) IDEA '97 also gave lip service to getting more parental involvement. Finally, teachers and administrators can now report criminal acts by students with disabilities to law enforcement officials, but the court judges fare little better than teachers and administrators at knowing how to discipline.

It's not just the advocacy groups who oppose changing IDEA in any way. The courts also hesitate to take up such cases unless the schools can prove a life is in danger. Please understand–the courts were taught by this very education system. The reasons given by the courts are that the disabled already have low self-esteem and long suspensions or worse punishment will only harm that already-low self-esteem.[9] The apple doesn't fall very far from the tree when a state-run teacher teaches a child who grows up to become a lawyer or judge. A criminal's self-esteem seems far more important than punishment.

The opposition wants a strong IDEA program so that no one is expelled. Such a plan certainly takes mainstreaming to its next level. If these groups have their way, mainstreaming will move from teaching severely handicapped students in the same classrooms as regular students to teaching murderous students in the same classroom.

Do you know who your children's classmates are?

&

AT LEAST ONE PRESIDENT LIKES THE IDEA

In 1997 President Bill Clinton signed a reauthorization of IDEA with some amendments that serve to benefit the government school officials and teachers. You might wonder if he got bad information when you read the following quote because he indicates that IDEA is improving disabled children's success. The only other explanation would be that Clinton could distort truth to make government look better, which we know he'd never do. "[E]very American citizen is a person of dignity and worth, having a spirit and a soul, and having the right to develop his or her full capacities. Because of IDEA, disabled children all over America have a better chance to reach that capacity. . . . We are saying that we do not intend to rest until we have conquered the ignorance and prejudice against disabilities that disables us all."[10]

GET 'EM WHEN THEY'RE YOUNG

A governmental proposal has been made to identify learning disabilities in children at the toddler age. The Department of Education fully supports this program.[11] Federal, state, and local government-supplied money is massively poured into Headstart and other preschool kinds of systems. Obviously, if the Department of Education can get toddlers before the children are old enough to enter Headstart, even more funds can be requested. Therefore, the search for disabled toddlers seems to be their next goal.

The question of how state bureaucrats could be given access to examine your babies is not clearly answered. Is a house-by-house inspection of babies to be administered? Once learning disabilities are found (trust me they *will* be found), it seems to me that these state officials will need to take your baby out of your home for a few hours a week of pre-pre-school special education. If they look you in the eye and say, "I'm from the government, and I'm here to take your baby so we can help it," you need to consider how you will answer.

REVEALING THE TRUTH

My wife Jayne taught special education in the government school system before she married me. Her take on some of the dangers of special education and public education in general is eye-opening indeed.

She taught for two years at an elementary school. The school was known as "one of the best." Keep in mind that most parents think the public school they send their kids to is "one of the best." Jayne's school was known specifically for higher standardized test scores than many other government schools in the district, so this "best" had apparent qualifications to justify the bandied-about title.

When you look below the surface, however, those qualifications for the best standardized test scores deserve a failing grade.

The school had a large special education program with Jayne's classroom called the Learning Disabilities Resource Center and three self-contained emotionally disturbed classrooms also in the school. Jayne explained how mainstreaming worked at the time. Once individual testing indicated that a special education student showed problems in one or more areas, that student would be sent to Jayne's classroom for those subjects. For example, if a special education student had trouble only in math, the student would be pulled from the regular math class and spend the time in Jayne's classroom to get math instruction there.

Jayne recalls how many problems this could cause other classes because the students often had emotional issues as well as subject problems, but they still went to all the other classes. They would sometimes disrupt the other classes they attended, creating chaos and hindering the learning environment for the more advanced students in the other classes. As long as the special education students attended Jayne's classroom and as long as Jayne filled out all the proper forms required by the government for her students, everybody was happy, and the impact on the other classes posed no concern for most involved.

The IDEA was that those special education students would be mainstreamed as much as possible. If they could have mainstreamed those students for all the classes, the system probably would have done so in the name of "self-esteem." They could not mainstream 100 percent of the time, however, because the schools have to justify why they receive added special education funds. Therefore, the paperwork and special classrooms and special sessions must be adhered to. To a cynic, the rules might appear to be far more important than the outcome.

The truth about how corrupt the government education system can be was made crystal clear at Jayne's school and probably most others when it came time for annual standardized tests that each school must administer. *The administration and faculty did not want one special education student to take a standardized test.* Some regular students' parents also expressed concerns about the special education students taking the tests because it would lower the overall school scores and thus would negatively affect the school's district and citywide rating. The school had a reputation to protect! Mainstreaming is fine as long as it damages only students, but the moment the school's reputation was at stake, they immediately tossed mainstreaming out the window. Even if a special education student was sent to the special education classroom for a single subject such as spelling but did okay in math and other subjects, that student was strongly discouraged from taking the standardized test that "normal" students took. Again, the stated IDEA's goal of making all students seem equal is once again proved to be a falsehood in reality.

These students did have to be given a yearly test called the Peabody Picture Vocabulary test, but *these results would never be included in the school's public standardized test averages.* Doing that would make the school look worse than the school wanted to look. Parents had to keep hearing that the school scored high in standardized tests because other-wise they might want to remove their kids from the government school system. Parents should never have a reason to do that because jobs, programs, and money are at stake. What about accuracy, you ask? You're worried about accuracy when positive financial publicity trumps accuracy in virtually every government school in the nation?

We later learned that Jayne's situation was normal and not an aberrant occurrence. Daniel Losen of the Harvard Civil Rights Project writes:

> Many suspect that poorly performing students are sent to Special Education either to exempt them from state tests or to explain a school's poor performance. The perverse incentive is to push kids out of your classroom to raise your test scores.[12]

To further the lie of so-called mainstreaming, Jayne was discouraged from speaking to her students in the hallways because this could identify them as special education students around others. Whereas the regular classrooms had bulletin boards outside of each class showing completed work done by the students in those classrooms, Jayne was not allowed to post her special education students' work outside her door. Even inside her own classroom, Jayne could post completed work on a bulletin board but no child's last name could appear on the paper. Mainstreaming is supposed to help regular students integrate and better understand special education students, but how can this happen when the special education students are barred from displaying their work where regular students are allowed to?

THE "BLACK HOLE" OF SPECIAL EDUCATION

Linda Schrock Taylor is an unusual special education teacher. She wants her children to leave her programs. If that happens, she sees it as a success. Her principal seemed to want something else. When she surprised her principal by releasing three special education students back into the normal education stream, her principal showed shock and concern. When she was ready to release a fourth student from her special education program, an evaluation meeting for that release was held without Linda's knowledge. The outcome is predictable: the student was placed in another teacher's special education program.

Taylor calls special education for disabled students a "black hole." Students fall in and are never to be seen again. She says the problem is rarely mentioned or discussed. Regarding special education, she writes: "Every year, thousands of our children disappear into the vagueness of special placements, never to be released from the labels and stigma; never to escape and again be seen as "normal."[13]

Even more damaging to these programs, paid for by federal funds and now Medicaid, Taylor writes:

> The most shocking and inexcusable aspect of the pretense, the mouth-service, given to "accountability," is the dearth of professionals who actively attempt to get students OUT of Special Education. Few see any value in specifically structuring Special Education programs towards 'repairing' and releasing children; few feel any urge to commend an exiting child; few see the importance of choosing curriculum and methods that would prevent the need for such programs in the first place.[14]

Out of 191,064 special education students in the state of Michigan during the 1999-2000 school year, Taylor shows that 185,248 returned the following year. (These figures do not include speech and language impaired students who often get one-on-one training until they can successfully communicate. The speech and language programs, even though they fall under the category of special education, do see quite a bit of success and graduation of students back into the regular student population. Part of that success may be attributed to students reaching an age level where their previously-slowed speech and language skills improved automatically as happens in some kids with such problems who literally grow out of them.)

Taylor does explain that severely handicapped students might not ever escape the special education curriculum. Certainly, that is understandable given the system's self-perpetuating actions. What is not understandable is how so many other students are labeled as "disabled" and never exit the income-generating special education programs. Like early ADA proponents who created millions of disabled out of nowhere, the educational system seems to do the very same thing. To further the premise that I've already put forth earlier in this chapter, Taylor confirms, "We must consider the possibility that these 'disabilities' are actually being created, within the confines and structure of the schools, by inferior teaching methods, and/or materials."[15] The mainstreaming concept seems to want to keep the special education labels. Once the children are labeled, their education and their future tunnels down the black hole that Taylor describes, never to be put back into a normal classification. As my evidence in this chapter shows, the desire for more and more funding is the sole cause for the rising number of disabled students each year.

Robyn Miller, a former government school teacher, further clarifies her view of this situation: "When I was a public school teacher, I used to think the system caused 75 percent of all learning disabilities. Now I think it's about 99 percent."[16]

Miller now teaches her children at home and spends much of her time warning others about the school system in which she herself used to teach. Her paycheck was less important than exposing the system, so one must admire her. She describes how in the so-called "best schools," the deteriorating social fabric continued due to higher and higher combined doses of political correctness and Ritalin.

RACIAL PREJUDICES

African-American students are often misdiagnosed as having mental disabilities. In America, black people account for 16 percent of the total student population and yet 32 percent of mild mental retardation students in education are black.[17] This racial discrimination is almost as severe as the abortion industry that murders two black babies for every three that are born.

One black student named William Walden did well in school but talked a lot and had a slight speech impediment. The school told William's mother that he was mentally disabled although they never would give him tests to prove their allegations. Such a test would show their diagnosis was wrong, and they could not risk that exposure. William's mom refused to sign papers needed to enter him into a special education program so school officials threatened to call child-protection services.

Insight magazine has told William's story and how his mother rescued him from the government schools after the third grade. He since graduated with a 3.9 grade-point average from a D.C. Catholic high school, and his mom now works for a group that promotes vouchers for poor children who need to be put in private schools where they might learn and not be discriminated against because of their color.

William describes the process:

> What they do is they intimidate parents. They come to you and tell you all these terrible things about your children, and then you feel compelled to sign the papers to put them in special education. Most parents don't realize that, once they're there, they're there for a long time. Especially with black males, they're there forever.[18]

♿

MY QUESTION FOR ATTORNEYS

Shouldn't all public school graduates use the Americans with Disabilities Act to file lawsuits requesting damages due to the disabling public school education they all received as children?

DRUGGING JUNIOR

Much has been written on drug addiction inside the public schools. This drug addiction is not learned outside on the playground by illegal dealers giving your kids their initial fix; the drug addiction is started and encouraged by the school faculty and administrators. If your child is labeled with ADD (attention deficit disorder) or one of the other disorders being bandied about in greater and greater numbers yearly, clinics are now springing up around America that will help get your older children off their Ritalin addiction that many of them may have formed by high school graduation.[19]

The schools send mixed messages to children. They say don't do drugs, and they drug the students daily. Spanking is illegal in the schools. Without spanking, a lot of children become totally unruly, so the schools drug the students into submission.

The sad truth about these behavior-modification drugs such as Ritalin and problems such as ADHD (attention deficit and hyperactivity disorder) is that the basis for their existence seems to be derived from extremely faulty studies. In addition, the benefactor of the drugging of school children appears primarily to be the mental health industry.

Ablechild.org is a Web site devoted to parents who want label-free and drug-free education for children. The labels this site wants removed are the "alphabet soup" of ADD and ADHD and all the other problem monikers that schools tag children with. (I often wonder if students know this alphabet soup of acronyms better than the real ABCs.) Ablechild.org describes the origins of these behavioral schemes:

> On September 29, 1970, a hearing was held before a subcommittee on Government Operations entitled: "Federal Involvement in the Use of Behavioral Modification Drugs on Grammar School Children of the Right to Privacy Inquiry." This hearing not only confirms the lack of validity of ADHD, but it also outlines the conflict of interest the Mental Health Industry has in the clinical research studies that it markets to the American people.[20]

The attention deficit-related and hyperactivity-related disorders appear then to have a false foundation. The mental health industry and not the students derive the benefits from drugging children if the results of this subcommittee hearing can be believed. Therefore, the entire matter of attention deficit-related disorders and behavior modification drugs should have been dropped in 1970, but they continue to be administered.

But as Milton Friedman has pointed out, public policy usually spins 180-degrees from its intended goals. The schools—astoundingly but predictably—adopted an approach exactly the opposite of the sensible one: assume the behavioral problems are accurate and assume that they can be dampened with drugs. Ablechild.org describes the results three decades later:

> On September 29, 2000, exactly thirty years later, Patty Weathers testified before a subcommittee entitled "Behavioral Drugs and Our Schools." Patty testified that her son was dismissed from the public educational system because of her refusal to continue to drug him at their request. Ms. Weathers has united with parents across the country that have lost their children from the harmful side effects of the drugs, as well as parents who refuse to label their children with unproven mental illnesses.
>
> Today, we have over 6 million children on psychotropic drugs. What started with clinical drug trials on children, without proper informed consent, has become a way of life in public education today.

The results are disastrous. As many as 5 million American children take Ritalin and other behavior-changing drugs. Despite the growing negative press, socialists who love to force themselves into others' lives often give the following reason: "If it saves one life, isn't it worth it?" But deaths directly attributed to these medicines range from seven to sixteen children each year.[21] For the first time, I agree with the socialists; I say we should shut down the programs immediately because if it saves one life, isn't it worth it?

Do you want to take drugs off the street? Perhaps you should encourage the government to look in places other than the seedy areas of your town. Economist Gary North describes how to get people off hard drugs by going to the source: "Where do people first learn this destructive behavior? Usually in tax-funded schools. The drug emporium of every neighborhood in America is the local public high school."[22] Although North was referring, at the time, to the schoolyards full of drug abusers and pushers, such a statement achieves more ominous meaning when school-sponsored Ritalin is brought into the picture. North's solution? Close the government schools. That sounds reasonable.

Falsely-diagnosed behavioral problems which are treated with drugs injected throughout your child's entire career would seem to be severe enough problems to catapult parents into action. But for some reason, most parents don't act.

For those who do keep their children in the government school systems (there are mysteries in life that will always escape my understanding), it will be incredibly difficult to protest when schools label your child as learning disabled and begin administering drugs. Some parents in Albany, New York, had to put their son back on Ritalin when they attempted to take him off the drug and get it out of his system. A family court (I use that term loosely) ruled that they had to medicate him for his ADD.[23]

The public schools are starting to cry "Child abuse!" when parents balk at the drugging of their children by government-paid strangers. According to Karen Thomas, a writer for *USA Today*, judges are beginning to agree with the school's child abuse accusations more and more.[24]

To help alleviate unwanted parental backlash, government handouts and Social Security Insurance (SSI) are now being made available to parents who have children diagnosed with ADD. Some parents enjoy the extra funding so much that they are beginning to request that their children be labeled as ADD. In addition, adults are learning that ADD is considered an adult disability too—under the Americans with Disabilities Act. Adult attention deficit disorder (perhaps the acronym for this would be AADD) is filling the void so that adults can now receive preferential treatment in the workplace when no physical handicap exists. In many ways, the schools are successful at creating the kind of society they set out to achieve.[25]

HOW PRO-CHOICE ARE YOU?

Parents have two choices if they do not want to expose their child to such lunacy as mainstreaming, IDEA, and lifetime Ritalin addictions: private education or home schooling.

Both private and home school options are better than public education in every conceivable aspect. Private schools, especially some religious ones, have such a heart for wanting to help children that they sometimes accept severely troublesome students who no longer participate in the government school system. If you consider a private school for your child's education—and you should seriously consider it—you need to talk to other parents of private schools in your area to help ensure that the school you choose successfully instills the education and morals that you want for your child.

For parents, lack of money is often an issue. Supposedly parents send their children to public schools for free. But not only do many of their tax dollars pay for that public education but the tax dollars of their friends and families also pay to educate their children for "free." Often Christian parents say they cannot afford to tithe, yet they tithe their children to the state six hours a day. To me, that is a far more costly tithe than the price of private or home education (which is basically free).

The cost of private schools is two fold. To send their children into a private school to be properly educated costs parents many dollars. Yet those parents do not get their property and income taxes back that the government takes for education. This double-taxation puts a stranglehold on many families who might otherwise privately educate their children. I implore you once more to consider that more is at stake than money. If your children are the most precious gifts you have, you would want to do everything in your power to keep drug pushers' hands off them. You would want to do everything in your power to keep strangers from falsely telling your children they are disabled. If your children truly do have handicaps, then you especially would want to keep others from exploiting those handicaps for personal and financial gain.

A word of warning is in order for parents who favor voucher programs for private schools. The voucher program is supposedly designed so that parents can send their kids to either a government school or a private school of their choosing. The private schools can take the voucher to the government to get money for that child; this is the money that would otherwise go to the public school if the child went there. Many private schools properly refuse all government money and say they will not accept vouchers if the voucher system becomes available in all fifty states. When a private school accepts federal and state money, either directly or in the form of vouchers, these schools are private in name only. When a private school accepts vouchers, the private school accepts strict federal guidelines for how the school operates and what is taught in that school.

For the purposes of this book, one of the most critical concerns is that the Americans with Disabilities Act imposes controls on private schools that accept federal money in any form.[26] For example, John Flanagan taught at a private Catholic school just when they were beginning to start ADA adherence. He was stunned that they were even considering the ADA. As he learned more about it, he wrote: "I've found The Octopus. It's the ADA."[27] When told that the ADA requires individualized education for each child, he continued: "Combine heterogeneous grouping with ADA, and private schools will, by dint of misuse of a paucity of funds, dumb down to avoid litigation."

Private religious schools that refuse government payments are generally exempt from the ADA although non-religious private schools must fully conform to the ADA. Some states such as Minnesota have adopted laws they term "Human Rights Acts" that in effect, extend ADA requirements to religious institutions as well as other kinds of institutions although fortunately most states have not followed suit. In your quest for a good private school, make sure the one you pick does not and will not accept any federal money of any kind. You then will be able to look your child in the eye when you teach her or him not to steal from others because you won't be stealing from your neighbor to pay for your child's education.

Max Victor Belz is a grain dealer from Grundy County, Iowa. As with many business owners, Belz can discern truth. He clearly understands the importance of protecting his children: "I don't want my children fed or clothed by the state, but I would prefer that to their being *educated* by the state."[28]

A SMALL CLASS SIZE IS VITAL, THEREFORE . . .

Nearly everybody agrees that class sizes need to be small for children to learn well. On that I can agree with the Department of Education officials who publicly utter that line every time budget proposals are due. Thus, the best education for your child is the smallest classroom setting possible: home.

If your child is disabled and I mean truly handicapped in some way—not just an easily exploited case for extra special education funds—then perhaps home schooling sounds like too much of a challenge. If that is true, I urge you again to re-read this chapter's earlier pages. Isn't your precious child who has handicaps important enough that you want to protect him from the hands of nameless, faceless Department of Education officials, administrators, and state-trained teachers?

Let me describe a study conducted by Dr. Steven F. Duvall from Kansas, published in the *Education & Treatment of Children* journal. Duvall found that home schooled children with learning disabilities do better than in special needs programs in the government schools.[29] Duvall's study showed that home schooled students get ten times as much one-on-one instruction as they do in the government schools.

During the study, home schooled students with diagnosed learning disabilities gained six months of reading education as opposed to two weeks of gain in the government schools. In writing skills, the home schooled students with diagnosed learning disabilities gained eight months of such education as opposed to two and a half months for those in the government schools. The study found that math results were comparable in both settings.

The parents had no education degrees. I suggest this fact contributed dramatically to the parents' abilities to teach. Two of the twenty home schooling parents had not graduated from high school.

If you hesitate to home school because you don't think you have the ability to teach your disabled children, I strongly urge you to reconsider in the light of Duvall's study. His study makes perfect sense. Who is more qualified to teach a child: a loving mom and dad or government-trained teachers with government-approved degrees getting paid with government money whose primary concern as you've seen in this chapter is to keep the government money flowing? Most parents who home school today thought there was no way they would be successful when they began. They now say they would not consider any other alternative.

If you worry about your child's socialization in a home school setting, you owe it to your child to visit a family of home schoolers. Generally, home schooled students look adults in the eyes, speak in complete sentences, have happy countenances, are polite, and seem to genuinely enjoy life. Many public school students who have been socialized by the government schools look at their shoes when an adult speaks to them and mumble one-syllable answers while wondering all the time why an adult is speaking to them. Your home schooled children will *not* be socialized the same way government school students will, and you will be exceedingly thankful they did not receive this socialization when you see the results.

Many times, my wife Jayne and I have been at a restaurant or some other public location when I've pointed children out to Jayne and said, "They are home schooled!" Her first response is, "How would you know that?" Then she sees what I saw: the children are polite, happy, smart, well-mannered, and respectful. After every prediction, I've asked the family if they home school. One hundred percent of the time I have been correct. The difference between a typical home school student and a typical government-trained student is astounding.

If your child is handicapped in some way, the benefits will multiply even more. You and only you know what your child needs and what is best for him or her. Don't let the ADA pass your child to IDEA to monitor things then pass your child to behavior modification drugs then pass your graduated special education child into the workplace to cry Adult ADD so he gets special treatment at work.

Many resources are available for parents who home school. If you doubt that you can home school, the Robinson home school course is a good place to start.[30] Robinson's course is a complete K-12 education that your child takes by himself with virtually no involvement on your part. The cost is $195, plus you supply a few math books from elsewhere when the curriculum tells you it is time to do so. That is the cost of this K-12 education, $15 per year averaged across your child's K-12 education. Your cost is $15 per year versus several thousands of dollars that the government spends per child in the public schools.

In addition to the Robinson course, the almost 2 million homeschooling families in America have found several other courses which are as effective although perhaps not as inexpensive as the Robinson course. Consider some recent education statistics for home schoolers in America:

- Two spelling bee champions in four years from 2000-2003.

- The National Geography champion and runner up in 2002.

- First-time four-medal winner at the 2002 International Mathematics Olympiad.

- Home schooled students are beginning to be highly sought by universities who have been wasting a tremendous amount of resources offering remedial English and math classes for incoming publicly-schooled freshmen.

In events such as the national spelling bee where a home schooler didn't win the top place, the per capita number of home schoolers who compete in the final rounds dramatically outnumbered public school and even private school students competing. In other words, home schooling students comprise a tiny percentage of the population of students, but a large percentage of them end up in the final rounds at so many of these mental competitions.

At $15 per child per year versus $7,000 that some states spend in school per year, a cost of 466 times more than a home schooled child using the Robinson curriculum, you must truly sit back and ask yourself if the public school's education is 466 times better than a home school education.

No argument is available that can show public school children generally get a better education than home schooled children. No study has ever shown that. The home school students score in dramatically higher percentiles on standardized tests such as college entrance exams. Yet, home school can cost as little as 1/466th as much as a public school education. The next time your local community wants to raise property taxes or start a lottery or pass a bond issue "for the schools," a reasonable question on your part would be to ask why they need more per child than 466 times the cost of a successful home school education.

TOO HANDICAPPED, TOO BUSY?

When talking to parents about home schooling, especially those who already send their children to government schools, parents frequently say they simply don't have time to home school. Life's too busy! Perhaps both parents work all day, and there's no energy at night for the kids. I always wonder why two paychecks are more important than successful, happy, drug-free, and label-free children, especially with such wonderful self-teaching home school curricula available.

I do understand that some families have problems that make home schooling more difficult. A family dealing with a handicapped child who needs some extra attention at times can certainly detract from the desire to home school.

In our neighborhood, one home schooling family comes to my mind when such barriers are raised in a conversation. I often think about this family of four whose hard-working father overworks himself in multiple jobs so that his wife can be the primary home school teacher for the kids, one boy and one girl. The mom has lupus which results in frequent hospital stays and weekly medical appointments. The son has a brain tumor. The daughter has neurofibromatosis.

Picture this family in your mind. Do you think the pressures in life that your and my families feel will ever come close to the *daily* pressures in this family's life? People often say I'm an encouragement to them. People often tell me I'm such an example for others who are born with physical problems. Let me clearly state that I do not know the definition of the term "problem" compared to this dear family of four. Every time in my life that I have seen anyone from this family, they have had a genuine smile, they have exuded a love for life, and they have glowed with a happy countenance.

Yet this family could not conceive of turning over their precious children to the state to be taught. They would not think of giving the most prized gifts in their lives to strangers to be poked, prodded, drugged, and destroyed. The battle of lupus is far less of a problem for that mom than a "free and easy" government school education.

You can educate your children better than anybody else. If your children have handicaps, you definitely can educate your children better than anybody else. If you have troubles in life that make you think you cannot home school, trust me, you can successfully home school your children if it truly matters to you. And it should. Do not let them be turned into special education money trees.

8

THE ADA VS. THE FREE MARKET

The ADA symbolizes a "freedom" based on maximizing the number of legal clubs that politically favored groups can use against everyone else.
—JAMES BOVARD, *Freedom in Chains.*[1]

T hus far, *Disabling America* has displayed considerable evidence that the Americans with Disabilities Act takes a massive toll on America, not just in costs, not just in bottlenecking the courts, but by hurting the very people it purports to help: the truly handicapped.

Chapter Five, "Spreading the Burden: The ADA in the Workplace," explained just how ineffective the ADA has been since it was passed into law over a decade ago. The statistics are staggering on how fewer handicapped are working and how many more people are on the SSI disability payment roles, especially given the financial boom years of the 1990s. Yes, during the stock market and business expansion in the 1990s, technology enabled more people with true handicaps to be effective and efficient employees; even so, still greater numbers went unemployed than before the ADA's passage.

I suggest that, *without* the ADA, handicapped employment would have increased. Without the ADA mucking up the works, the free market would have been far more inclined to hire the handicapped (as it had done in the many years before the ADA was conceived). Post-ADA businesses can no longer scout for the very best employees for a particular position. The inevitable result is that America's companies are less efficient and offer less than superior customer service.

The DisabilityInfo.gov Web site lists the following areas from which people with disabilities can get government help:

- Employment
- Education
- Housing
- Transportation

- Health

- Income Support

- Civil Rights

TECHNOLOGY

The basic fact is that wherever government solutions abound, private ones diminish. The great American political thinker Albert Jay Nock called this the difference between state power and social power; because government is essentially legalized force, when the state flexes its muscles, social institutions and private individuals usually give way.

You can see this on the grand scale. Companies cease hiring the handicapped because their perceived needs are already being taken care of by the government and to hire them might only incur more costs. You can also see this on the small scale. With government offering so many services (however poorly) for the handicapped, families already pressured by jobs, high taxes, and so on, find it very easy to step aside and let the government provide. When the government begins to provide help, that is often where families stop helping each other. If a truly severely-handicapped person cannot function without twenty-four hour supervision, his or her family will almost always allow the government to come in and take over that care. The government encourages this by the very existence of its programs.

Today the punishment for being handicapped is that your family will turn you over to strangers, paid for by money taken from other strangers. I realize these are stern words. Our society has already, in large percentages, told elderly parents that the government will get them housing and care until they die, and now those same services are available for the handicapped. The family is then free to enjoy themselves guilt-free instead of providing the most important love and care they can offer their parents. In an ADA-free world where these kinds of government controls would not be allowed, freedom would ensure that families need each other and take care of each other.

LOOK WHAT THE ADA'S DONE

The diminishment of private-sector solutions has had terrible results. Employers hired the handicapped before the ADA in larger numbers. The Social Security Insurance roles had fewer handicapped people on them before the ADA. That's been established. The reason is simple: handicapped employees often make good employees. They've overcome a disability of some kind. Doing that builds character. Employers before the ADA knew this instinctively. One major cause for the increased SSI disability roles is the loosening of the definition of the term "disability" over time.

Edward L. Hudgins addresses this specific phenomenon when he says:

> Before the ADA many employers were inclined to hire handicapped individuals for jobs that would pose no major difficulties for them. Employers might reason that handicapped workers would be especially anxious to do good jobs, to prove themselves worthy of their tasks, to show that their disabilities are, in effect, no real handicap. McDonald's, for example, went out of its way before the enactment of the ADA to recruit mentally handicapped workers for its fast-food outlets.[2]

Notice that Hudgins begins these words of wisdom with, "Before the ADA." In addition, it's worth noting that the ADA has since thanked McDonald's for hiring the handicapped early on by sponsoring numerous lawsuits against them.

One of the most ludicrous lawsuits against McDonald's is worth noting. In 2003, Samantha Robichaud sued a local McDonald's franchise for refusing to promote her. She claims her lack of a promotion was due to her appearance.[3] Robichaud was born with a dark, purple birth mark that covered a large part of her face. Such a birthmark is known as a "port wine stain."

The reason this discrimination claim is especially absurd is because

McDonald's is known as one of the largest contributors to organizations that perform corrective surgeries and emotional support for children born with facial deformities. McDonald's says that it provides the funding for these kinds of charities because it wants to eliminate "emotional trauma and social isolation" that these problems can cause.[4]

Why would McDonald's want to spend hundreds of thousands of dollars over the years to help people overcome emotional trauma from facial problems and then completely do an about-face to discriminate against one of their own employees due to that employee's looks? McDonald's is the best-known fast food company on earth; they didn't get there by making stupid decisions like keeping an employee from a promotion due to the way her face looks.

♿

FREE MARKETS AND THE DISABLED

McDonald's certainly isn't the only company to implement help for their handicapped employees without coercion from the ADA.

On October 16, 2002, Wichita, Kansas, and eleven other Kansas communities participated in National Disability Mentoring Day.[5] The American Association of People with Disabilities (AAPD) and the United States Department of Labor sponsored the event. Normally when those two groups get together the free market understandably quivers from fear, but at this Wichita event, Bank of America and COMCARE were two of several private organizations that lent support and major funding for the event.

The sponsors provide mentoring to "mentees" who are described as being men and women who receive disability services. The mentors were volunteers from local organizations who help explain their professions to the mentees and help the mentees identify career paths they may be able to take. I have no doubt that these private organizations benefit as much as the handicapped who partake in the mentoring services. Such programs would probably be more numerous if the Americans with Disabilities Act didn't frighten away so many companies.

Now ponder this: Is it a prudent decision for McDonald's to continue hiring people who create hassles for them this way? Is it any wonder that *after* the ADA, fewer disabled are being hired than before?

RECAPPING THE DAMAGE

By now, you should understand how and why the ADA forced the following results that the free-market, unhindered by ADA, would have never brought about:

- More discrimination against the truly handicapped

- Increased disdain for the handicapped due to the cost business owners were forced to incur

- Fear of hiring the handicapped due to lawsuits backed by the U.S. Department of Justice

- False disability claims resulting in increased SSI payments and massive litigation

- Further deterioration of the government school system that was close to complete deterioration already

- Embarrassment of the truly handicapped for all that's done in their name

YET ANOTHER TARGET: RENTAL PROPERTY OWNERS

The fact that handicapped employees show added character and accomplishment in what they do is not enough to offset the ADA's damage to handicapped employees.

I know from experience that handicapped tenants often make superb tenants. Just about any rental property owner would be pleased to have them. I have authored one of the most successful books ever published about managing rental properties. I used to own and manage several properties, and my parents still own and manage many today.[6] If I had a choice to rent to a handicapped tenant I would prefer such a tenant selfishly, not out of guilt or because of some law, but because I know that such people who have overcome hardships and can live on their own are generally extremely honest and reliable.

If a handicapped person applied to rent one of my houses, I would bend over backwards to rent to that person assuming they met the income, rental history, and other standard requirements. If it meant building a wheelchair ramp, I would gladly do so. Proof that a disabled rental applicant overcomes the adversity that life gave her and is seeking to live on her own and has employment to pay the rent would show me a lot about that person's character.

Another landlord might not feel that way and choose not to build a ramp. Fine. That is his loss, and the tenant shouldn't want to rent from him anyway. That leaves more preferable tenants available to the more caring (and smarter) landladies and landlords who understand risk and return. The purchase of private homes and apartments by rental property investors and their selection of tenants represents one of the last bastions of the free market in real estate—that is, if you ignore the rent-control laws in areas of the country such as Manhattan.

But the ADA advocates simply couldn't allow the free market in rental housing to stand a moment longer without intervening.

In the name of protecting tenants, one Web site recommends adding the following to all lease agreements:

> Landlord shall promptly, at the Landlord's sole expense, remove any architectural barriers or make any modifications necessary to the leased Premises or the Common Areas as may be required by Sections 302 or 303 of the ADA. Landlord shall indemnify and defend Tenant and shall hold tenant harmless from any damages, loss or liability including without limitation the cost of barrier removal or alteration which may be performed by Tenant, resulting from the failure of Landlord to comply strictly with the requirements of the ADA.[7]

You'll note that this wording says the landlord will make *any* modifications necessary. More ominous is the phrase *without limitation* when discussing how much the landlord must spend for barrier removal and alteration of the property. I know of several rental property owners who provide nice, clean housing to tenants at just-under market rates (they've read my rental property book and know how to do this). They would leave the business immediately if they were faced with choosing between making unlimited alterations to their properties at the ADA's whim or selling their places. They would all be forced to sell. One makes money at rental properties over a very long period of time. On a month-to-month basis, the income is marginal and does not allow for alterations that incur costs as those *"without limitation"* would incur.

The epilogue of my own landlord experiences turned out not to be as positive as the first many years were. One of the reasons I left the business was due to the Americans with Disabilities Act. I had heard talk indicating that the local government was going to require visible smoke detectors in all rental properties. These detectors are for hearing-impaired people who may not hear a siren but who can see the strobe flash of the visible smoke detector when it goes off. These are costly devices at $100 plus when I looked into them. I saw absolutely no reason to replace all my current smoke alarms, two or three in each rent house I owned, just on the *chance* that *some day* a deaf person *might* rent from me.

When fewer private rental property owners like myself exist, the more the government will become everybody's landlord. The government has taken over being the father of millions of children, and this action causes massive abuse, poverty, and crime. Now the government seeks to make itself everybody's landlord: the one who sets the rules. Thus, renters will face much higher rents in much lower-quality housing. The private solution, tailored to the actual needs of the individual tenant, gets battered by the ham-fisted rule of government that winds up hurting everybody in the long run.

If a deaf person were to apply for one of my houses, I would more than likely jump at the chance to rent the property to that person. I would replace those smoke detectors within two hours of my agreement to rent the property to that individual. But I refuse to be forced to spend almost an entire month's rent replacing all the smoke alarms with visible strobe-based smoke alarms in all my places when none of them had deaf people living in them. I believe that criminal extortion is against the law only because the government does not like competition.

At this point, the local requirement for visible smoke detectors has not been enacted. The requirement for them in all rental properties has not yet come to pass. But the future does not look promising.

BOY SCOUTS HONOR AND HELP THE HANDICAPPED

The Nashville Predators and the Wilson County Homebuilder Association lent their financial support to an Eagle Scout project that Will Crawley designed and wanted to build. Will is an eighth grader with a mild form of cerebral palsy. This fourteen-year-old had met an eight-year old girl who told him how she would love to play in a tree house, but she would never be able to do so due to her wheelchair confinement.

Will pondered and then decided that a tree house the girl could enjoy would make a wonderful Eagle Scout project. Others agreed and publicity grew. Will not only designed the house but also solicited funds from companies close by. A local fraternity and the Homebuilders Association helped Will construct the tree house. The tree house was built for the Empower Me Day Camp, a nonprofit organization that serves disabled children. The tree house has a raised deck for wheelchairs and spans two trees. Ramp access was built into the structure to enable any child to play in the tree house.[8]

Will Crawley is just one of thousands of Boy Scouts who has made an impact for good on handicapped people's lives. The Boy Scouts play a large role in teaching normal kids about handicapped children and integrating the handicapped into their programs. Eagle Scout projects often involve building wheelchair ramps or trails so the handicapped can have more options. One New York Boy Scout Council helped a school of severely disabled children learn to identify and locate insects for a science project. The Council also built camping equipment for handicapped children who wanted to enjoy camping and provided transportation for elderly and disabled parishioners in local churches.[9]

As might be expected in today's America, the Scouts are often denigrated for their acknowledgement of God in their oaths and their patriotism, as well as other preferences such as their lack of desire to recruit homosexual Scout leaders.

The Boy Scouts are major players in promoting the idea that each person can find his strengths and overcome obstacles. Ten-year-old James Milam exemplified exactly what the Boy Scouts promote when he got down from his wheelchair and crawled from grave to grave at the Nashville National Cemetery for Memorial Day Weekend in 2003. He placed an American flag on each American soldier's gravestones to honor those who died for America. He used a ruler so the flag he posted at each grave was exactly one foot from each headstone.[10]

Without the ADA's "help," the Scout programs have been and will remain independent promoters of freedom, ability, faith, and knowledge of right and wrong. They show a desire to help the handicapped live the most complete lives possible through their projects as well as through their many programs for their own handicapped Scouts. The Scouts do have some troops set aside with severely handicapped Scout members. But the Boy Scouts of America Web site indicates that, in addition to these special troops of boys with extra needs, many handicapped Scouts take part in regular Scout troops. Like a loving family that successfully integrates its handicapped children into the larger family, the Scouts state that:

> The basic premise of Scouting for youth with special needs is that every boy wants to participate fully and be respected like every other member of the troop. While there are, by necessity, troops exclusively composed of Scouts with disabilities; experience has shown that Scouting usually succeeds best when every boy is part of a patrol in a regular troop.[11]

Such examples of private-sector successes with overcoming handicaps and helping the disabled abound, despite the ADA. Doubtless they would flourish without it. When the government forces a kind of mainstreaming as found in the schools, as opposed to letting individuals and organizations handle the disabled the way they see best for their situation, mainstreaming corrupts and harms the handicapped as the previous chapter demonstrated. When free enterprise sees a benefit of mainstreaming in a particular instance, the free market has the ability to predict its success.

THE BLIND NOW WATCH MOVIES

Jim Stovall is nationally known for several reasons. He was a national Olympic champion weight lifter. He worked as a successful investment broker. His entrepreneurial skills earned him the coveted 1997 Entrepreneur of the Year award. He received the year 2000 Humanitarian of the Year award. He is a sought-after motivational speaker and author. He co-founded a national television network of which he is now president. He hosts a national talk show called *NTN Showcase*. He works behind the scenes on several movies and television series.

Jim Stovall is also blind. When Jim was seventeen, a degenerative eye disease took away his sight.

Jim's success story is astounding, but so are so many other stories of people who overcame physical disabilities without any help from the government. Jim found his success not just in one arena but in many that have touched so many people.

In spite of all he has done, Jim is best-known for the movies he makes. Jim makes it possible for the totally blind to see . . . movies. He makes movies for blind people. More accurately, he takes movies already made for the sighted and transforms them into movies the blind can watch also.

Some ideas are so obvious and so simple and solve so many major problems that such solutions fall under most people's radar for years and are never thought of. After going blind, Jim had one of these ideas that probably should have been, but was not, invented long before.

Jim Stovall takes movies, mostly older classic films with high standards and morals, and adds a soundtrack with a narrator telling all that happens. The normal soundtrack and dialog are kept in the movie. The end result is that you might find one of his movies speaking to you saying, "*[And now Joe walks over to the mailbox, he opens the lid and drops his letter in looking weary as he does so.]* <Honk!> *[Joe jumps as the car startles him.]* 'Joe, I haven't seen you in a while!' *[Joe turns to see his sister, wearing a bright red coat looking happy to see him.]*"

Isn't that a brilliant idea? Don't you wish you thought of it first? I wish I had.

These movies are really amazing if you have ever seen them. Stovall saw a void in a market. Stovall filled that void, gave hundreds of thousands of blind people the ability to watch movies they could never have understood fully before, was rewarded financially by the movies' success, and even people who are not blind enjoy them! Over 60 percent of his audience is comprised of fully-sighted people who take pleasure in watching his productions.[12]

You may recall from Chapter Two that ADA advocates sued the AMC Entertainment movie theater chain for not providing wheelchair seating on the upper decks of their auditoriums. I'd rather not give these pundits more ideas, but I do worry that perhaps they'll now try to close the Blockbuster chain for not carrying movies that the blind can watch. Sometimes I think the ADA fans will only be happy when they have closed every business in America. If they do go after Blockbuster, they should instead target Hollywood, the primary culprit, for it is they who make these non-accessible movies. There is no fear of an ADA advocacy group going after the Hollywood industry though, given how both groups seem to cherish and promote socialism.

THIS LITTLE LIGHT HOUSE OF MINE

In 1970, Phil and Marcia Mitchell gave birth to a precious baby girl. The doctor informed the Mitchells that their newborn would be severely visually impaired and be legally blind. Knowing about other blind people who overcame their hardship, the Mitchells would not accept anything but full opportunity for their daughter to enjoy life. They immediately began to seek a school that would be able to train their daughter in skills needed for life when she got older.

Although schools for the blind existed, many of which were funded by American taxpayers, the Mitchells did not want to rely on the state for their salvation. Being strong Christians, the Mitchells wanted to put their faith in God to provide the answer that was best for their daughter.

Marcia Mitchell found what she was seeking, although the answer was not what she originally expected. She and another mother of a blind child, failing to find a school they thought would fully honor their faith, opened The Little Light House in Tulsa, Oklahoma. From three blind students and one teacher, The Little Light House now provides education, with a full ministerial emphasis, for a full range of severely physically and mentally handicapped children. The tuition cost to the families of these severely handicapped children is absolutely zero. The Little Light House has run on donations from the public since its inception. In 1990, they were able to build a new 22,000 square foot school facility at a cost of $2.2 million dollars. In their thirty-year history, the school has remained completely debt-free.[13]

What makes The Little Light House so unique among many other institutions like them is that The Little Light House refuses all government funding.

The Little Light House is not just an example of the free market working before the ADA. The government was there and willing to help financially when The Little Light House opened its doors in 1972. The Mitchells knew that when the government helps, the government controls. The Mitchells required a free market solution because they saw, accurately, that to whom much is given much is expected.

The school is not just known locally. The Little Light House is one of the most widely recognized and admired severely handicapped educational locations in the world. Not only did the free market produce the result, the Mitchells would not have allowed anything but the free market to create their dream of The Little Lighthouse. The Little Light

House received the "Presidential 1,000 Points of Light Award" in 1991. In the three decades it's been open, The Little Lighthouse has changed the hearts and lives of countless students, families, volunteers, donors, faculty, and staff who have had the pleasure to be involved. People come from around the world, some to educate their children and others to see how faith can move mountains.

One only needs to look today at the life of The Little Light House's very first student, Missy Mitchell, to see if The Little Light House can train a child well. Missy Mitchell went onto receive her music education degree from a major Oklahoma university and then became a sought-after recording artist in the Christian music industry. Missy continues her work winning awards, providing inspiration to all who hear her, and being a beacon of light to those who can see as well as those who cannot.

DISABLED SHOOTING SERVICES

In what must be an anathema to many who support the ADA's existence, in my opinion the most successful non-government program to assist the handicapped is the Disabled Shooting Services at the National Rifle Association (NRA).

Handicapped gun enthusiasts, collectors, target shooters, and hunters can obtain comprehensive help from the NRA. That help includes everything from locating shooting ranges close to home that are wheelchair accessible to getting advice on equipment they can use to hold their guns and shoot better. The NRA sponsors numerous competitions where handicapped shooters compete in national tournaments. Government game and fish agencies have actually contacted the NRA's Disabled Shooting Services division for advice in dealing with hunters and fishermen who need extra help. (Those game and fish agencies would not get much ADA support, I would assume, if they called the ADA hotline instead of the NRA. The United States Department of Justice is not very friendly towards a person's inalienable defense right to keep and bear arms. Even for the one-armed.)

The National Rifle Association was the first national shooting sports organization in the world to devote an entire department to shooters with handicaps without the need of government bureaucrats and lawyers forcing them to do it. They hired the foremost experts on disabilities and shooting sports to solve the challenges handicapped shooters face. Dave Baskin has been the manager over this NRA division since its inception. Baskin is now considered to be one of the world's most acknowledged experts in the field of disability-related shooting sports.

Dave Baskin once gave me some expert advice. I told him that I enjoyed shooting of all kinds but mentioned that I couldn't shoot high caliber revolvers because the shape of my hands won't enable me to hold such guns firmly but that I had no trouble with shotguns, rifles, and semi-automatics. In twenty seconds he told me how to overcome the revolver problem. He said that any leather smith could create leather gloves for me, with the proper construction of Velcro straps that would enable me to shoot any revolver I cared to shoot. Such a simple solution never occurred to me. Of course, it occurred to Baskin because he is expert in this very matter.

I'm not the only shooter who appreciates the NRA's services, as the NRA describes in one of its older articles on this special division:

> [In 1994,] NRA Disabled Shooting Services received over 2,500 phone calls and letters for information and advice concerning various shooting sports issues. The services varied from designing adaptive techniques and equipment that assisted hunters' return to the sport they enjoy, to developing shooting programs for physical therapists to use in the recovery of their post-injury patients. This NRA Rehabilitative Shooting Program has drawn worldwide recognition.[14]

This laudatory statement was made years ago. The NRA Disabled Shooting Services division has seen tremendous growth and outreach ever since. The NRA-Beeman Grand Prix Championship is the premier disabled shooting event in the world, and in 1999, the NRA-Beeman tour set the all-time shooting sports record for one-day paid attendance at 23,250 in Cleveland, Ohio.[15] The NRA is now staging shooting competitions in foreign countries for the handicapped. Even anti-gun nations such as Canada and Ireland welcome the Disabled Shooting Service competitions due to the good will they bring and the interest in the handicapped shooting competitions they sponsor.

Women have been encouraged to play major roles in the National Rifle Association for decades. In demonstration of the NRA's support for women and their right to defend themselves, the Disabled Shooting Division also sponsors women-only and mixed shooting competitions between men and women.

Although the government, attorneys, and ADA advocates still struggle to understand what a disability really is, the NRA had no trouble in developing standards that fit one's handicap into a shooting competition that works best for that individual. The NRA classifies shooters based on their ability to function as opposed to dwelling on what they cannot do. The NRA wants all handicapped shooters to be able to compete fairly no matter how varied the handicaps might be. So the NRA created sets of standards and categories covering different shooting requirements and different possibilities for the many forms of handicaps possible. For example, the NRA-Beeman competition accepts two primary categories of shooters that may further be broken down depending on the circumstances: those in the SH-1 class who are safely able to operate a rifle or handgun without any adaptive support and the SH-2 class who require some adaptive equipment.

As a service to my readers who may be interested in learning more about this program, I suggest that you call the NRA's Disabled Shooting Service division at (703) 267-1495.

DISABLED SELF-PROTECTION

Some readers may be startled by the previous section. Guns are dangerous, after all. Should handicapped people be allowed to shoot them? Let me tell you one argument I've heard: A handicapped man or woman could very easily misfire a gun, perhaps even shoot themselves, so guns should be kept as far as possible from them. The desired result, as far as I can ascertain, is that the handicapped should not have the right to defend themselves.

Advocates for the disabled (which I often note seem to be comprised of a huge percentage of anti-gun and anti-defense zealots) do what they can to turn the handicapped into victims, overstating discrimination against them, and even telling stories (I chose that term carefully) about massive numbers of attacks against the disabled simply because they are disabled. If the disabled are attacked so frequently, why can't they have the added protection that a weapon can provide? If the ADA advocates were honest, they would require that the ADA buy every disabled man, woman, and child in America a gun so they would have a more equal chance at defending themselves. If you think that will happen any time soon out of love for the disabled, you probably still believe there were 43 million Americans with disabilities in 1990.

If I'm handicapped and I cannot defend myself against an attacker as readily as a normal person due to my physical differences, then it's an accurate definition of "equal access" for me to be able to carry a gun— it levels the playing field.

The gun issue is actually a perfect example of government solutions trumping private ones to the detriment of the handicapped. No solution to a problem could be more private than defending *myself* with *my* gun. But anti-gun advocates would rather I rely on a police force that probably cannot help with my being mugged until I stumble into the police department office with a broken nose and an empty wallet.

Possibly all this agitation from anti-gunnners could have a rosy side. If I'm handicapped and I cannot defend myself against an attacker as readily as a normal person due to my physical differences, then it's an accurate definition of "equal access" for me to be able to carry a gun. Let me preview a related concern that has brewed in the back of my mind for a few years: The government has more than once hinted at requiring gun locks for weapons in the home. This legislation would make it illegal to own a gun that did not have a gun lock in place. Such a lock requires a key or combination that unlocks the gun to use it. The anti-gun, anti-constitutional Congress and other crowds that promote mandatory gun locks need to be careful. In my opinion such a move will violate the Americans with Disabilities Act. The disabled cannot unlock those gun locks as quickly as normal people can. Therefore, we'll be put at a distinct disadvantage when the time comes for us to defend ourselves.

Although I cannot conceive of using the ADA ever in my lifetime to get something I wanted, if the mandatory gun lock crowd and the U.S. Department of Justice ever get their way concerning gun locks, I will be thrilled to pit one governmental set of lunacy laws against another set of lunacy laws. Sue the Department of Justice over required gun locks by using the Department of Justice ADA regulations as justification for the suit. Perhaps one can overcome the other and getting rid of either one would be a battle truly worth fighting for. If it eliminates one government agency or law, isn't it worth it?

9

THE ADA AROUND THE WORLD

The Austrian Supreme Court has ordered Casinos Austria to refund nearly $3,000 to a compulsive gambler. The court ruled that the country's leading casino chain did not "investigate the man's financial situation and therefore neglected its obligation to protect its clients." Critics believe that the ruling opens the door for a stampede of losing gamblers attempting to prove that they're pathological in an attempt to recover casino losses.

—Las Vegas Advisor, February, 2003.

O bviously, the Americans with Disabilities Act is only concerned with America. What I have seen in my extensive world travels, however, is that, just like its culture, America exports its legislation. Other countries are adopting measures similar to the Americans with Disabilities Act, following the U.S.'s lead. The result? The same as here: Hurting the handicapped populations in the name of helping them.

Other nations' disastrous attempts to wrangle with handicapped-related laws and regulations also have potential influence on our ADA. Some of these regulations in the name of the handicapped are so terribly bad for these nations and for their handicapped people that the cynic in me feels for certain these new-and-improved ideas will be part of our Americans with Disabilities Act as soon as our advocates can implement them. For example, if a compulsive gambler ever successfully sues a Las Vegas casino for his losses, the gaming industries of Nevada, Atlantic City, the riverboat casinos around the country, and the Native American casinos, as well as others will close their doors when people clamor to recoup their losses by claiming a gambling disability. Whether you believe gambling should be legal or not is not the issue here because such a closure of such a massive industry (not to mention state-sponsored lotteries) would be a disastrous economic gut-punch.

Please bear with me while I recount my findings from other countries. Some of these situations will shock you. More worrisome, a fight is continuing between the United Nations and America over sovereignty. America has acquiesced some of its sovereignty of self-governance to the U.N. in the past, although unlike many who fear such things, I do not see us as acquiescing enough to make a huge difference in Americans' lives so far. Yet we do seem to move closer to a situation in which the United Nations will govern more and more of our lives. In the context of *Disabling America*, I want to give you a preview of the plans the U.N. has for the world's disabled population, thereby exposing some troublesome issues. Through that exposure, maybe their "well-meaning" enslavement of the handicapped can be delayed somewhat.

TRAVELING FOR HANDICAPPED PARKING

When you travel to a busy European city such as Rome or Athens for the first time, you are shocked right away at the parking situation. The people park *anywhere* and *everywhere*. Along the streets you might still see traces of painted parking lanes from the past; the locals appear not to see these. Double-parking and triple-parking, especially at night, is only the beginning. A wide thoroughfare through Rome's *Monti* district, for example, is so clogged by parked cars that a driver is fortunate if he can find a single lane open even though the street was constructed to have two lanes in each direction plus parking strips on the side. Making matters worse, locals also park their cars on the sidewalks—right in front of stores and all through alleyways. Often to walk down a street in the evening, you have to walk in the single lane that's left in the middle of the street because you'd never make it around all the cars piled up on the sidewalks next to the buildings.

In the first few years that we visited Italy, this phenomenon was one of our highlights: seeing how they'd park each evening. No tickets are given because the situation is just so chaotic. Even supposing someone wanted to park legally there are no legal spaces available, only pieces of them as three or four cars park harum-scarum across whatever resembles designated parking spaces.

Starting about 1995, Jayne and I noticed that the Italian government implemented a change. Wheelchair signs and painted handicapped parking spaces appeared on streets about every fifty yards. The Italian people have big hearts, but the outcome has been fruitless.

Those signs may have made the bureaucrats feel good, but not one empty handicapped parking space can be found in the evenings; even during most days, there's not a single car parked in them with a handicapped permit. Yet, the officials did something—namely, *nothing*. In Italy as in America, the process is far more important than the results when it comes to handicapped regulations. The Italian police know full well that nothing else can be done. There is absolutely no means to enforce those spaces; so the signs go up, but it's still business as usual: chaos. (By the way, Italians pronounce their word *caos* very close to the way we pronounce *chaos*—they understand this word very well!)

I only wish Americans got away with parking in handicapped spaces when all other spaces are full. The ADA police are far less reasonable than the Italian *Carabinieri*.

AMERICA EXPORTS ADA TO THE WORLD

In May of 2003, Secretary of Labor Elaine L. Chao urged her international audience of disability experts to take this clear and concise step towards helping the handicapped: "Continue to bring focus and awareness to solutions that insure the full inclusion of persons with disabilities into the 21st century workforce."[1] In other words, nothing substantial will be done to help the handicapped, but you can be sure that those *employed* to help the handicap will benefit.

Chao made her speech at the "Pathways to Work in the 21st Century: A UK-US Seminar of Exchange." Chao told the group they should "improve employment opportunities, transportation options, and assistive technology systems for persons of all ages with disabilities." It frankly makes me sad to see this being propagated around the world with such silliness as requiring people of every country to pay for assistive devices for everybody who needs them. At the time of this writing, the world economy is generally recessed. Meanwhile these leaders continue to push for disability legislation that will further erode economies.

PRISON HIV COVERED

AIDS activists in America use the ADA as one weapon in their arsenal. As we export ADA to other nations, other nations find their own ways to create and enable the disabled; AIDS provides one avenue. In Cape Town, South Africa, an ex-convict sued the government because he got AIDS in prison. We can only hope that this South African story does not portend what may take place soon in America. The ex-convict sued the South African government for 1.1 million rand (about 132,000 US dollars) saying that he got HIV from another inmate during his one year in prison. The reason he sued the government is not because they failed to protect him from a rape; he sued the government because they failed to supply free condoms and warn inmates about the dangers of unprotected sex. The ex-convict said that he "would not have had sex and, subsequently, contracted the virus had he known of the risk." The Department of Correctional Services changed their policy to provide condoms in 1996.[2]

WATCH OUT IN FRANCE

In Marseilles, France, Willemijn Forest bore a son with Down's syndrome. The doctors immediately asked her if she wanted to keep him or have him aborted. It's fortunate for Mrs. Forest that the doctors asked her because immediately following the delivery, they took the baby away assuming that she would not want to keep the baby.

She said that she was appalled by their attitude. "Of course I want to keep him," was her reply to the question of whether she wanted her own baby slaughtered.[3]

It appears that Amnesty International never protested this state-sponsored attempted murder. I could find no evidence that France's government went in to shut down the hospital due to their inhumane treatment of handicapped children. The American Civil Liberties Union (ACLU) who supports euthanasia (the killing of sick, old people) has not stated any objections to France's practice, nor has it warned America that it should protect the civil liberties of its babies. Hillary Clinton and other sponsors of the United Nations' "Rights of the Child" program have said absolutely nothing about the rights of *this* child. Most telling, not one Americans with Disabilities Act activist has called for a boycott of France or an investigation into France's euthanasia slant against the innocent handicapped. All of these groups mentioned believe that you should feed those who do not work such as winos and drug addicts but that you should not feed the sick, the old, or the comatose. Therefore, their silence on this French practice is to be expected too. When it becomes illegal to birth a baby with Down's syndrome in America or acceptable to commit outright infanticide, I predict their silence then will be deafening.

France strongly opposes the death penalty for murder. One might now assume that's because they would lose too many doctors.

The *Christian Science Monitor* says that to the French society "a disabled life is not worth living." France's highest court has ruled that Down's syndrome children have a legal right never to have been born and they may grow up and sue doctors who allow them to be born. In light of this, who could disagree that doctors are strongly encouraged to murder all such children? The handicapped child's murder is legal, but letting the handicapped child live can be grounds for a big lawsuit.

In another case, a woman was upset that her child was born with Down's syndrome. She was not upset at the disease but at the fact that the doctors did not tell her she was going to have a baby with that disease. She would have aborted the baby immediately. Now, she collects governmental financial aid for the baby's care, but she wants the doctor to assume 100 percent of the cost to raise her child. She blames the doctor for letting the baby be born.[4]

In a historical footnote to France's current experience, Adolf Hitler, the man who enslaved France in World War II before America and her allies liberated the country, had a personal physician who wrote a paper calling for the legalization of euthanasia to kill the sick, handicapped, and elderly.[5] How's that for ironic?

♿

A DISABLED BY ANY OTHER NAME

The Swedish Tax Authority monitors what parents want to name their children; since some names will lead to discomfort, they must approve of all names that parents want to name their children. The discomfort from their unsavory names might give the children a complex, perhaps even lower their self-esteem.

Therefore, the Swedish Tax Authority deems it necessary to step in and save the child from a life with discomfort. When Johan and Sara of Goteborg, Sweden, wanted to use Staalman for the middle name of one of their sons, the Swedish tax authority told them that name would harm the child. Staalman is Swedish for Superman.[6]

Ask yourself what boy on earth wouldn't want Superman for a middle name. There is not one boy on this planet whose self-esteem would not be multiplied ten-fold with such a name.

If the name police come to America's disability advocates, something tells me that biblical names such as Peter, Paul, Mark, Joseph, and Mary would be one of the first set of names our government ADA officials would ban.

INDIA PROTESTS FOR DISABLED RIGHTS

Many groups around the world study America's disability model and are fighting for such a system in their countries. Typically, they want to go even further than the measures established in America.

In 1995, India passed their Disability Act, a law which supposedly instilled "a ray of hope in the disabled population."[7] According to the Disability Act, all public places should be made accessible. Also, the private sector is required to employ 5 percent disabled people within its total workforce. For one– and two-person shops and market kiosks, one wonders what has to be done there to ensure the 5 percent rule is adhered to. By 1999, many companies did not employ a single disabled person. If only the ADA advocates had been there to teach them how to turn normal people into "disabled" the way they have so successfully done here, then the quotas could easily be met.

A Disability Right Group (DRG) issued a press release on the seventh anniversary of the passing of the Disability Act stating the following:

> The disability sector, to a fair extent, has been successful in nego-
> tiating with the Government and public sector for equal opportu-
> nities for disabled people. Unfortunately, due to the sluggishness
> of the private sector, this issue has not been taken seriously.[8]

Certainly government bureaucracies are the same the world over. A government will always fail to understand the concept of limited resources and the optimum use of funds. All governments with a central banking system, like America, can print their own money and tax as much as needed. Many tax increases are hidden in property tax assessment increases and licenses and fees collected through regulatory agencies. The Indian government used its unlimited taxing ability to fund these projects that appease these disabled advocates. The private sector struggles to make ends meet (in India especially), so it will obviously lag behind the government when forced to install costly changes. But, as in America, what do agitators care about the costs of business?

If the American government were to analyze these stories around the world, it could perhaps study why these plans fail and take measures here to keep the same mistakes from happening under the auspices of the Americans with Disabilities Act.

Pankaj Kapoor from a group called the Action for Abilities Development and Inclusion (AADI) said the following: "Jobs are limited in [the] private sector for the disabled. Even if jobs are provided, there is an accessibility problem. I am on [sic] the wheelchair. If I get a job in private sector, will they provide accessibility to me?"[9]

I sincerely hope that Kapoor gets a job. I want him to be a productive citizen in India. Yet, my first thought upon reading his lament is that if he is an effective employee, he would already be employed. No company is going to let a wheelchair stand in the way of hiring a good employee. A company's honorable pursuit of profit means they would be willing to spend what it takes to get any good employee who will work for them. I would rather Kapoor work harder at getting a job himself than rely on his government to get him something. Worse, the government's quotas truly make Kapoor into a pawn. The government uses Kapoor and others like him when they make demands such as this: "You *will* hire more disabled workers until you meet your five percent quota, and we may not even allow you to hire a non-disabled worker until you meet your quota!"

So far, the Indian government's enforcement of this regulation obviously lacks much punch given the deficient adherence by many businesses. Whether the Indian government's disability stance continues to be one for show or turns into one of force remains to be seen. I suspect that the recent and dramatic increase in worldwide demand for Indian labor, especially in the high tech area, outweighs India's desire to enforce draconian measures which could reverse this current economic growth.

A WORLD ADA? JUST SAY NADA TO A WADA

Without major fanfare from the national media outlets, September 6, 2000, saw further erosion of America's self-governing sovereignty. The United Nations hosted the United Nations Millennium Summit. People often scoff that America would ever turn over any of its sovereignty to an international organization such as the United Nations. But the goal of governing the world, however, is a primary goal for the United Nations. Listen to Maurice Strong, co-chairman of the U.N. Commission on Global Governance who stated, "It is simply not feasible for sovereignty to be exercised unilaterally by individual nation-states, however powerful."[10]

Of course, just because a United Nations chairman supports world governance doesn't mean that America is going along with it. Right after that statement, however, Strobe Talbott, the United States deputy secretary of state at the time, strongly confirmed those very words: "Nationhood as we know it will be obsolete, all states will recognize a single, global authority. . . . National sovereignty wasn't such a great idea after all."[11]

The United Nations Millennium Summit put the following items on its primary agenda:

1. A global peacekeeping force (Code for American troops being placed under UN leadership).

2. An International Criminal Court (Code for eliminating what little is left of the death penalty and other effective criminal-eliminating punishments).

3. A global tax system (Code for America funding the world).

4. Redistribution of wealth on a global scope by requiring wealthy nations to give money to poor nations (Code for America giving even more money to nations classified as "third world." More third world countries are announced each year. Of course, if the UN had at all been effective in its fifty-year history, there would be *fewer* third world countries each year, not more).

5. A global approach to AIDS (Code for the United States giving millions or billions of dollars in the name of AIDS worldwide).

6. International gender-mainstreaming (Code for promoting a worldwide radical feminist agenda, a notion that Planned Parenthood passionately supports due to the income it generates in worldwide abortions).

7. International public education (If you think the American schools are bad now. . .).

8. International affirmative action (arbitrary hiring quotas) and an international minimum wage law.

9. Complete absolution of past debts from poor nations (Code for America not collecting debts owed to it by smaller nations who promised to pay it back when we loaned them the money at their request).

10. Implementing an international version of the Americans with Disabilities Act (To guarantee that third-world nations remain third world).

I include this complete list of items to show you the company the ADA keeps. The United Nations appears to be proud of the job that America did with its Americans with Disabilities Act. As with anything else the United Nations does, if it implements a global ADA-like system the results will prove disastrous. The U.N. clarified its position on disabilities, leaving no confusion as to where they will push the global community:

[Governments should] recognize the special potential of people with disabilities and ensure their full participation and equal role in political, social, and cultural fields. To further recognize and meet their special needs, introduce inclusive policies and programmes for their empowerment, and ensure that they take a leading role in poverty eradication.[12]

UNABLED WHEN DISABLED

The United Nations has produced a Web site entitled, "United Nations Enable," or as I call it, Un-enable. The Un-enable site proudly displays the phrase "United Nations Persons with Disabilities Web Site." The site's stated mission is this Orwellian phrase: "To assist in the promotion of effective measures for prevention of disability, rehabilitation, and the realization of the goals of *full participation* of disabled persons in social life and development, and of *equality*" (italics theirs).[13]

To socialists, the search for equality is akin to the search for the Holy Grail.

The site dictates "international norms and standards" that countries should follow to adhere to the Un-enabled guidelines for accommodating the handicapped. Before listing any norms and standards though, Un-enabled goes through several lines of rhetoric taken straight from the ADA originator's playbook by stating how discriminated against the disabled are and how they are denied their basic civil rights. Worth extra attention is that the United Nations felt compelled to include a section there called "Convention Against Torture" just to engender more pity before spouting their disability decrees. The disabled agitators who created the ADA failed to think of the torture angle when they were trying to justify the ADA's passage; just think how much mileage they could have gotten by tossing in the word "torture" when they discussed how America victimized her disabled.

Most of the site is the usual, ominous, United Nations gobbledygook that says very little specifically so they will be able to enforce whatever they want to enforce. Yet the fact that they are getting organized on the Un-enabled site should cause concern. They are not just giving speeches now but they are organizing their actions and deciding the best approach to tyrannize countries into paying up.

The most striking item to me about the Un-enabled site is, on its main page, they list "Gender and Women with Disabilities" as one of their top five priorities. It seems to me that they are prioritizing helping women and people who can't figure out their own gender ahead of everybody else (basically that means ahead of all men in the world). The United Nations likes to discriminate on the basis of gender, and you can see this in virtually every action or statement it makes. It's more important to the United Nations that women and gender-confused disabled individuals get what's coming to them before the rest of the population's disabled are to be considered.

CONTROL FREAKS VS. CONTROL FREAKS

When one government agency wants to violate another government agency's regulations, generally nothing happens unless it costs the second agency money. For example, if someone's rights are trampled by a government agency as opposed to a private company, the civil rights people often avert their eyes to let it occur because there is little money to be made by litigating.

This appears to be true the world over. The state-run security staff at Australia's Adelaide Airport over-scrutinized the sixteen-year-old handicapped students in wheelchairs who had just competed at the Twelfth National Junior Games for the Disabled.

Similarly, another Australian teenager got a civics lesson in governmental regulations recently at an Australian airport. Kathleen O'Kelly-Kennedy is Australia's tallest basketball player. The fact that she wears an artificial leg seems not to be an issue in her life. Great for her. The airport officials made it an issue, however, when they forced her to remove her artificial leg in front of dozens of other horrified passengers.[14]

After the incident, Kathleen said this:

> It is quite clear when I lift my pants that I wear a leg prosthesis. I also had given it a few whacks so there was no doubt that it sounded like a false leg. It was too much that [the] security staff then chose to frisk me, from ankle to hip, in front of dozens of other passengers. I had already taken my shoes off, which made standing difficult, and I was not even offered a seat.[15]

Kathleen describes her shakedown as an experience that made her feel like a criminal. She added this: "Wherever I go, I know I will always be a bit different, but I don't let it affect me. But what happened on Sunday puts my difference in a whole new and negative public light."[16]

She is exactly correct. Not only were other passengers probably embarrassed for the girl, but some were undoubtedly even angered that she had an artificial leg. It slowed down the line! Like the man who yelled at my friend Janice for parking in a wheelchair space before he saw her spend ten minutes getting her daughter in the wheelchair to take her into the store, arbitrary government regulations often cause tremendous friction where none existed before. Some who were running late for a connection probably were angered at Kathleen. Yet it is this intense scrutiny of law-abiding citizens who never fit one terrorist profile that creates an atmosphere of anger. The ADA does the same thing.

If you've been through security at any airport in America or elsewhere in the world since September 11, 2001, you too have been scrutinized and publicly fondled in the name of security. But you have been especially scrutinized if you are black, white, Asian, or any of the many other racial or ethnic categories that have not been shown to cause global-wide terror. The refusal to profile the groups of people most likely to commit terrorist attacks based on obvious statistics will generate anger where anger would not exist without such draconian measures. In addition, it will force people such as Kathleen to be dramatically embarrassed. No Australian disability counselor will be there because doing such a strip search of the handicapped takes no money away from any disability program.

It's not been that bad for me, but it's getting close. I am almost always taken aside and patted down. I must always remove my shoes and often raise my pants so the pat-down teams can feel what they want to feel on me. I must say that it's not just my leg that causes me concern when I fly. As an extensive world traveler, I have a permanent American Airlines Gold status giving me special privileges such as upgrades and early check-in among other things; flying for a Gold member is often much easier than for regular passengers.

I typically took thirty to fifty flights each year for over a decade before September 11, 2001. Since that day, I have flown one time on a paid ticket. Being treated like a criminal at the airport made me promise myself that I would never again fly on an airplane if I paid for the ticket. My artificial leg makes them first assume I am a criminal before they assume I am a customer. Even if I wanted them there (which I don't), no ADA official is there to ensure they treat me the same as everybody else. My flying days are over.

I have since flown, but it's been to use up the numerous free airline miles I had saved over the years. Once they are gone, I doubt will ever again fly if I must pay for the ticket. The airlines complain about hard times, and they blame the lack of passengers on fear. I assure you I have no fear of terrorism. I simply refuse to be assumed a criminal in the security lines. With an artificial leg and with an Americans with Disabilities Act that could not care less about true handicapped discrimination, the airlines must be made to realize they have to put pressure on the airports to change security measures to include profiling of those groups who have committed terrorist acts and to stop treating law abiding citizens like criminals. If the airlines go bankrupt before they realize this, so much for them.

A CHANGING WORLD

I often wonder which is worse: America exporting all its ills, such as the ADA, to other countries who implement such foolishness or America importing foolishness, such as its seeming acquiescence to the United Nations, an organization that wants to control lives worldwide and make America the primary funding source for that control.

When it comes to disability regulations, America leads as the primary exporter. The world has only begun to change. The future looks bleak for the world's disabled if ADA-like advocates are spreading throughout the globe. Most readers of *Disabling America* will be Americans, and America's disability regulations are still evolving in ways you may not have imagined. In the next and final chapter, I give you my preview of what you can expect in the ADA-controlled America over the next few years.

10

Your Future with the ADA

With crutches everyone has questions, but not with a cane. With crutches it's a funny story; with a cane it's a sad story.

—George to Jerry, *Seinfeld*

I began this book by describing how unfair the Americans with Disabilities Act is to the truly handicapped. I stated that equal access is impossible. The ADA, for example, does not require that doors be wide enough for bed-ridden patients. In 2001, George W. Bush, son of the President Bush who signed the ADA into law, described the New Freedom Initiative:

> My Administration is committed to tearing down the barriers to equality that face many of the 54 million Americans with disabilities . . . . My New Freedom Initiative will help Americans with disabilities by increasing access to assistive technologies, expanding educational opportunities, increasing the ability of Americans with disabilities to integrate into the workforce, and promoting increased access into daily community life.[1]

I see very little more that can be done to "increase the ability of Americans with disabilities" unless bed-width door openings are soon a requirement for every business and bathroom in America. I don't see that happening (and I hope it does not). Equal access truly isn't what the ADA is all about, a fact that is evident throughout *Disabling America*.

The Americans with Disabilities Act threatens to grow even stronger. While the ADA has stung public and private organizations, a few areas are left where the ADA has yet to sink its teeth. But things may change. In this chapter, I will show you where those areas are. They will hit home with you. Literally.

This final chapter will also look at some of the ways the ADA has changed recently, as well how the ADA may affect your future in America. The Americans with Disabilities Act will probably get worse.

After all, the ADA has continued to get worse and worse since its origin. Reform is not an option–to improve the ADA means eliminating the ADA.

LOCK YOUR DOORS—THE ADA IS COMING

You might assume that ADA advocates realize the importance of private property and the importance of keeping regulatory hands off people's homes. Yet their actions do not support this assumption. In the mid-1990s, I predicted that, after going after private businesses, the Americans with Disabilities Act would soon begin to tell you how to build and adapt your own homes. That was one prediction I did not want to come true. But it appears that it has come true and is gaining momentum.

In 2001, the Santa Monica City Council wanted to increase "visitability" to private homes, as Larry Elder reported.[2] "Visitability" is code talk for forcing ADA-specific requirements on people's homes who live in the area. The Santa Monica City Council says that many friends of the disabled live in homes that have no accessibility. So the council wants the government to make friends of the disabled install expensive ramps and grab bars and widen their doors.

Elder writes about Santa Monica's rent control laws. He says that these laws result in "below-market rent whose tenants drive BMWs while their landlords drive Hondas." The rent controls are not the only controls on the City Council's agenda, as we see from their bullying use of the ADA.

Alan Toy who sits on Santa Monica's Rent Control Board and has polio reveals one reason for the desire to force private homeowners into spending tens of thousands of dollars: "I'm one of those people who thinks community rights supercede property rights."[3] Many in the former Soviet Union felt the same way.

It's a shame that Toy suffers from polio. It's also a shame that misery loves company and he seems to want all his friends to be miserable. I can think of no other conclusion to such a statement that is so damaging to the very society that allows him to make such unwise statements, threatening the very ties that hold communities together by using the power of government to coerce his neighbors and friends to live as *he* requires them to live.

Toy is not alone. Mary Ann Jones has been confined to a wheelchair and crutches for thirty-two years. She says the proposed Santa Monica requirements are vital "because we can't go see our friends." With friends like her . . . . Ironically, Mary Ann Jones is the Executive Director of the Westside Center for *Independent* Living. Not only do such requirements oppose the very ideals the Founding Fathers built America upon, and not only do such requirements remove people's inalienable rights to be free to own and live on whatever properties they desire, such requirements are highly costly to homeowners. Regulations such as the ADA already cost American people billions through taxes, increased prices, and lawsuits against private businesses, but such regulations will now directly impact the price of housing dramatically.

John Schaub, real estate investor, explains in detail what takes place with these kinds of regulations:

> What drives prices of homes higher and higher? Several factors [including] the increasing government regulation of both land developers and builders. When I first began developing land in the 70s it would take me about six months from the day I bought the land until the day I could start selling lots. That time has increased to more than three years in my town, making the risk and carrying costs dramatically higher. Likewise, builders today have several times the requirements and regulations than builders of a couple of decades ago.[4]

I want to return to one ADA requirement for business and see what you think about this requirement in your own home. Round doorknobs are illegal. Look around your home and count the doorknobs you will be replacing if the advocates turn America into Santa Monica. Levered doorknobs are costly, as much as twice the cost of round doorknobs.

(Simple toddler locks do not work on them, so young parents, watch out.) You might have scoffed ten years ago at the notion that the American government would require you to remove every round door-knob in your house. After the previous chapters in *Disabling America*, you certainly can no longer scoff at that. To what extent are you willing to go to become compliant? I will go to jail before I make my home ADA compliant by state coercion. What a comedy of errors that would be: jailing a handicapped person because he refused to comply with the Americans with Disabilities Act.

On June 10, 2003, Jan Schakowsky, Democrat from Illinois, introduced HR 2353 which is called the "Inclusive Home Design" bill. I would have named it the "Intrusive Home Design." The law will require all single-family homes receiving federal funds to be built with a no-step entrance, thirty-two-inch clearance doorways on the main level, and one wheelchair accessible bathroom.[5] The problem here is not that ADA is putting its nose where it doesn't belong but that federal funds are being used to build homes. Only active military personnel should live in federally-funded housing. The ADA only compounds the problem.

HR 2353 does portend what's coming to your home. It appears already to be in your neighborhood because, on June 3, 2003, the George W. Bush White House attorney, Theodore B. Olson, urged the Supreme Court to acknowledge that sidewalks are covered by the ADA.[6]

FREEDOM FLUSHED

In a way, the ADA has already entered your home along with another monster set of environmental regulations. When both the environmentalists and the ADA advocates team up to get you, they get you.

Around the time of the ADA's signing, Congress passed a law that required all new toilets to use less water than previous ones did. Every toilet built and sold in America since that decision has been far inferior to the ones most of us grew up with. Managers of new hotels can attest to how the new toilets (I call them *toylets*) have incurred frequent repairs from stoppages and overflows. Water damage can be costly to repair. Perhaps the toilet plunger industry at least has benefited from this new requirement, but no one else has. Sure, it's a dirty subject, but someone's got to keep exposing these foolish attempts to control your life.

The law of unintended consequences hits most environmental regulations just as it does ADA regulations. Users often have to flush the new toilets a number of times where before, a maximum of two and generally only one would do the trick. These new toilets consume far more water in the long run than the old ones.

When Jayne and I moved into a new home a few years ago, only *toylets* could be found. I didn't want wasteful governmental regulations to enter my bathroom. As a steward of my family's income and as someone who does not want to pay for extra water we didn't want to use, I went on a mission to seek toilets we could still purchase that did not waste several gallons of water at each use. I found the perfect toilet. It met the government's regulations of using much less water but had air-pressurized tanks that used air to move the water through the system much more efficiently. Instead of a flimsy handle on the side, they had a heavy-duty push-button in the center of the tank lid that put immediate downward pressure on the flushing mechanism to ensure positive flushes each time. In other words, they worked even better than the golden era toilets! We placed our order and they arrived– without the superior flushing button. Instead, the plumber messed with the handle for about two hours trying to get the side handle to start the flush mechanism. We had to have him back repeatedly, and the toilets never flushed properly. Not once. The air-pressure mechanism was great but to activate that mechanism, a regular side toilet handle could not utilize proper leverage.

I was on the phone immediately asking why I could not get the one kind of power toilet that worked: the kind with the push button on the top of the tank lid. I was told, as I should have expected, that someone challenged that button under the guise of the ADA. The advocates said that people with deformed hands would be unable to flush using the buttons. No advocate asked *me* if that were true– they made the decision for me. Instead of allowing the option as a choice, ADA advocates and most others on the "pro-choice" Left do not like you to have *any* choice in *any* matter. They ruled the pushbuttons out. The flimsy style of side handles are what we're left with. America is left using toilets without enough water powered by handles that are inferior.

ATTACKING THE PRODUCTS YOU BUY

Once the ADA advocates control the way your home looks, with ramps coming from your driveway posted with a handicapped parking sign and a painted wheelchair space in front of every one of your doors, I can think of another area of life where the ADA can get to you and control what you do and how you do it. Although there are no indications yet that this will happen, I believe it's a real possibility that the Americans with Disabilities Act could be expanded to cover the very products you buy. You saw a preview of this disaster in the previous section when they outlawed toilets with flush push-buttons that worked so well.

Should a regular hammer be available for sale in a hardware store where someone who was born with only three incomplete fingers might see the hammer? His self-esteem may be hurt, according to ADA doctrine. Perhaps such hammers should be hidden behind the counters and sold in plain brown paper bags so that those with deformities in their hands won't become depressed. (I own about six hammers and use them regularly when I work in my barn and around my acreage.)

If the advocates do begin to attack the very products you buy, saying they either need to be made more accessible to the disabled or they need to be eliminated altogether, perhaps then the truly handicapped will speak out against such lunacy.

THE INTERNET IS NEXT

There is still another place that the ADA wants to control: cyberspace.

All government Web sites must conform to a new standard so that they are considered to be more accessible. This means few pictures, text in a format for text-reading software, and a design that allows for simpler navigation by some disabled. Tim Berners-Lee, the inventor of the World Wide Web (no, Al Gore did not originate the "www" that precedes most Web addresses) said this about the Internet: "The power of the Web is in its universality. Access by everyone regardless of disability is an essential aspect."[7] I fully agree with Mr. Berners-Lee in the spirit of what he said. But to make the Web fully accessible by everybody, every Web page must be designed with the lowest common denominator in mind. Instead of being free to have any color, for example, your site may soon have to conform to a specific color set so that color-blind people will have fewer problems. Freedom of expression and of ideas on the Internet is a wonderful blessing, but now the advocates want to tell you exactly how you will express your ideas. You will have a Web site if you design it the way they say. You must pay for it, too.

Such Web page regulations are not yet required, but the move towards such regulations is not too distant. The World Wide Web Consortium, the group that helps design, develop, and promote Internet standards, is working on their Web Accessibility Initiative. The goal of the WAI is to increase accessibility to both Web sites and applications such as your word processor and email program. They want to make the interface to the Web and other programs available for people with disabilities.

Such a goal is wonderful. The World Wide Web Consortium should make accessibility standards their priority. Site owners who want to adhere to none, some, or all of those standards should have them available so they can make the proper designs. The problem occurs when the advocates force the government to require these changes from you and anybody else who may want to put up and manage a Web site.

Already, on-line companies that do business with the government need to conform to some of these accessibility requirements such as moving text out of graphic images so that text-reading software can locate the text. If they want to keep their government contracts, then these companies must change their sites. This is extortion. Much worse is the future possibility that private individuals wanting to post a Web site of family pictures may not be allowed to post such a site until it is expensively converted to a fully accessible site.

Walter K. Olson has written the following about the harmful effects of ADA regulations on the Web:

> Web design creativity and spontaneity would be stunted, as publishers feel constrained to use only tools approved by 'official' bodies, and amateur websites would be winnowed as legal and technical rules limit the art to a professional's . . . Functionality could also suffer—the use of color to convey information, for instance, is problematic. And what about the First Amendment implications—can communication on the web be limited in ways unimaginable for newspapers or magazines?[8]

Once, the advocates tested how much control they could have over Internet sites when they sued Southwest Airlines in 2002 because the airline site violated the Americans with Disabilities Act. In court, the ADA advocates described Southwest Airlines as using its site for being an "exhibition, display, and a sales establishment."[9] All three of those words were offered to sour the court against the free market even though all three words in reality conjure the American fabric and free enterprise. Hitting the transportation sector when it was at a low point was a low blow. The advocates may have planned this attack when their new enemy, the airline sector, was weak financially. Perhaps Southwest Airlines was targeted because within the weak airline sector Southwest has been more profitable than all other airlines since September 11, 2001; therefore, it is better positioned to pay huge ADA damage and extortion awards.

Fortunately, the one place in all of the ADA's rules and regulations that ADA authors were not *vague* was what constituted public access. The ADA lists the following places where the ADA applies: an inn, hotel, motel, or other place of lodging, a restaurant, bar, motion picture house, theater, concert hall, auditorium, bakery, grocery store, laundromat, dry cleaner, and bank . . ."[10] The list goes on, but its authors did not include the Internet.

Therefore, the judge ruled that the ADA did not cover cyberspace and dealt the real blow to those advocates who spent money to bring the suit. Of course, Southwest Airlines was harmed financially by the mere act of having to defend against such a frivolous suit, as well as having to defend subsequent appeals the advocates are sure to go for.

The ADA rarely lets such a decision stand. The Americans with Disabilities Act's regulations will surely be changed to include the Internet. Whether such cases will hold up in court, well, the jury's still out on that one. Past evidence has clearly shown, however, that the odds are great the Internet will be dragged into the ADA's controlling grasp soon.

TECHNOLOGY ENABLES THE HANDICAPPED

To go after the Internet and computer industry, which has done so much for the handicapped, is truly a shame. The blind have incredible systems that enable them to "read" many Web sites, send and receive email, and control their computers. Physically-impaired people use computers all the time due to the many input devices that are available for them. Voice recognition systems—which are very accurate today and getting more so all the time—are aiding many. As paraplegic physics genius Stephen Hawking proves, one can write the bestselling physics book of all time, control a computer, speak through a computer's voice-generation capabilities, and maneuver a wheelchair with nothing more than a single straw-like input device. Hawking writes this about his experience with technology:

> David Mason, of Cambridge Adaptive Communication, fitted a small portable computer and a speech synthesizer to my wheel chair. This system allowed me to communicate much better than I could before. I can manage up to 15 words a minute. I can either speak what I have written, or save it to disk. I can then print it out,

or call it back and speak it sentence by sentence. Using this system, I have written a book, and dozens of scientific papers. I have also given many scientific and popular talks. They have all been well received. I think that is in a large part due to the quality of the speech synthesizer, which is made by Speech Plus. One's voice is very important. If you have a slurred voice, people are likely to treat you as mentally deficient: Does he take sugar? [asking another person at the restaurant table instead of asking the handicapped the question directly] This synthesizer is by far the best I have heard, because it varies the intonation, and doesn't speak like a Dalek. The only trouble is that it gives me an American accent.[11]

In spite of these colossal advances technology brings to the handicapped, from the free market alone, the ADA wants to control technology. Such control will surely slow down all advances being made.

&

MICROSOFT SUPPORTS ACCESSIBILITY

Microsoft has added voice-recognition and hands-free technology in its popular Microsoft Office System software. This technology is wonderful, and it enables Microsoft to put its software to use by many people who might otherwise not be able to use it.

In the late 1970s, without any coercion from the government, Bill Gates began one of the largest and the most effective anti-poverty organizations in the world: Microsoft. Microsoft provides food, clothing, shelter, and money through a mechanism known as "the free market." Handicapped employees can be seen throughout Microsoft offices all over the world. Companies that see the importance of helping the world using the company's own resources are to be commended. The result for the handicapped is that Microsoft has enabled so many of them to function with a computer where they could not do so without such help.

Regardless of these free-market advancements, government presses onward, enacting reams of new, unneeded regulations. On February 12, 2003, President George W. Bush signed an Executive Memorandum that established more costly ADA-related bureaucracy. The signing established the "Interagency Working Group on Assistive Technology Mobility Devices." (Speech-impaired people should look into suing ADA advocates for developing such long, complicated names.) This group is responsible for identifying existing federal government programs and resources that help them obtain and provide technology devices, such as mobility devices, that disabled people need for education and employment.[12] In other words, the government is paying for more and more services for the disabled and will require new technology to be developed. The free market can do this better and cheaper. The government has neither the ability nor the authority to implement these sweeping policies.

AUTHOR'S TIME OUT

While writing this book, I came down with Bell's Palsy, a viral infection causing complete paralysis of the left half of my face. Although the full effects typically last only three weeks or so, the shock of getting it was horrible, especially before I learned it is usually temporary. I found that my ability to use a computer greatly diminished. The computer is my workplace and has been the centerpiece of my career for years. A blow to the use of my computer is a direct blow to my family's provision.

My left eyelid would not close, even for sleeping. Not being able to close my left eyelid required constant drops and gels. To make the eye less sensitive to dryness, I wore an eye patch much of the time, but the diminished depth perception made reading text on my monitor quite a chore. Fortunately, I remembered that Microsoft Windows and Office have built-in text-reading software. When my good eye got too strained, I could make the computer read me text from emails and from the books I was currently writing. Although this software served me well, I found that I was not used to composing by ear. I write better (debatable by you, perhaps, my reader) when I see what I'm reading during proofing stages instead of hearing it read back to me.

My typing ability was also much diminished. Although some say I type at a fairly speedy rate, with my compromised depth perception, my typing slowed to a crawl. I also lost tremendous accuracy. One answer to typing problems would be voice recognition software, which I do have (once again, thanks to Microsoft although many companies provide similar computer technology to what I'm describing here). Even with the voice recognition software, I found that with the left side of my face paralyzed, my speech was so poor that my computer microphone picked up too many mistakes and I could not train the voice recognition software fully enough given my bad speech to make it worth the effort.

Therefore, from a personal experience I can say that the technology available to me with my new, albeit temporary, disabilities did help me considerably in some ways and much less in others. Having said that, I have seen numerous people, from the completely blind to paraplegics, who use computers and other forms of technology to make the computer perform far better than I was able to do.

When I taught computers at the college level several years ago, a blind student took my C programming course. C is a textual language that contains all kinds of special characters and does not allow for much ambiguity. I showed *my* short-sightedness to the blind student by wondering when the course first began how a sightless man could keep track of C code, especially given my long assignments. At the end of the course, he had a perfect score on every program and almost a 100 percent on all his tests. He utilized text-reading software to function better as a computer programmer than I will ever dream of doing. He was, at the time, a full-time computer engineer and programmer.

The combined resources of today's technology and human freedom conquer and triumph adversity. Toss in governmental regulations, and productivity, happiness, and efficiency will always be diminished. I do not want our post-ADA legacy to be a diminished America.

CHANGES IN THE ADA'S FUTURE

Other than the items I've put forth throughout the earlier pages of this chapter, some amendments and changes to the ADA have been passed in the recent past. I chose not to focus too much on these changes throughout most of the book because we do not know the impact of these changes and how the advocates will position themselves to take advantage of them.

Recent propositions, such as the ADA Notification Act described in the next section, indicate an attempt to keep the ADA from barreling its way further into destroying America through countless regulations and subsequent lawsuits. I have little hope for these changes because I see what has come before. The ADA is a monstrously large structure inside the United States Department of Justice, and its claws are entangled in virtually all aspects of American life in its first decade-plus. I suggest that to think some minor amendments called "reforms" will change anything so complex is simply naïve.

Having said that, I suspect this book will come under attack for my criticisms. Advocates and Web sites are in place to rid the nation of anti-ADA speak. ADA Watch is a Web site whose self-proclaimed mission is "to activate the disability community's grassroots in response to threats to civil rights protections for people with disabilities."[13] This is just one of many organizations that are diligent to stamp out opponents of the ADA. Such organizations will not care for this book and will probably lament how little the reforms being discussed over the years made their way into this book. I designed the book in just that way simply because we do not know the future; we only know exactly how the ADA and its supporters have damaged America so far. Without that background, it would be an unfair account to discuss ways it may improve in the future if it's only gotten worse since its inception.

THE ADA NOTIFICATION ACT

Clint Eastwood backs the ADA Notification Act, so it can't be all bad. Eastwood testified for this bill, HR 3590, to amend Title III of the ADA so that before filing an ADA lawsuit, a person allegedly suffering discrimination must provide a formal notice of the violation to the business. The plaintiff must then wait ninety days before going ahead with the suit to allow the business to make the necessary changes.

The ADA Watch Web site strongly opposes this common sense amendment to the ADA. If one truly wants compliance, and not just money from locating marginally non-compliant organizations, then one would approve of the ADA Notification Act. Yet the ADA Watch Web site says that this bill will: "Weaken civil rights protections for people with disabilities and create a disincentive for voluntary compliance with the ADA. Additionally, the legislative process will open up the ADA and expose it to even more weakening amendments."[14]

Let's hope their fear of further ADA weakening comes true. At the time of this writing, ADA Watch also states that the disabled community is united against this proposed legislation. Obviously, that is a false statement because I am for weakening the ADA through the ADA Notification Act. I wonder if the ADA Watch wants to respect my concerns as a disabled person? If so, they should amend their site so that they accurately say *not all* disabled are opposed to the ADA Notification Act.

THE ADA IS A COMPLETE AND UTTER FAILURE

In a stunning acknowledgement, the Center for an Accessible Society says this on their Web site: "In 1990, 70 percent of people with disabilities were unemployed, and the figure remains the same today [post-2000]."[15]

That "70 percent" figure does seem to exaggerate the number of unemployed disabled people in 1990, especially given the ADA's fallacious origins. But even if it is accurate, the amazing admission that 70 percent are *still* unemployed is telling.

If the Americans with Disabilities Act has done *absolutely nothing* to help employ the disabled, then *get rid of it*. Today by noon. Stop the erosion of American freedom. The definition of "solution" has never been that a status quo problem remains in place. The ADA is a complete failure that continues its work to bankrupt America's future and harm the truly handicapped.

APPENDIX

THE ADA IN ITS OWN LEGALESE

B elow is the principal text from the Justice Department's Disability Rights Section that forms the foundation of the Americans with Disabilities Act. The following text, taken directly from the ADA.gov Web site, is indicative of the larger ADA as it stands at the time of this writing, September 2003.

The titles and requirements set forth below are generally the titles and requirements directly quoted by ADA litigation experts when suing organizations for discrimination against the handicapped. Actual building specifications for the disabled are not included due to their overwhelming details. If you would like to see the ADA's requirements (mislabeled *standards* by its authors) for all construction and remodeling, you can download such a document here: *http://www.ada.gov/stdspdf.htm*. If you choose to download these ADA building requirements, I strongly suggest that you use a high-speed Internet connection; a 4.5 megabyte file will come your way when you access the file.

As for the material following, while reading through the ADA's requirements, consider how often these keywords appear: *charges, discriminate, discrimination, lawsuit, suit,* and *violations.*

AMERICANS WITH DISABILITIES ACT

The ADA prohibits discrimination on the basis of disability in employment, state and local government, public accommodations, commercial facilities, transportation, and telecommunications. It also applies to the United States Congress.

To be protected by the ADA, one must have a disability or have a relationship or association with an individual with a disability. An individual with a disability is defined by the ADA as a person who has a physical or mental impairment that substantially limits one or more major life activities, a person who has a history or record of such an impairment, or a person who is perceived by others as having such an impairment. The ADA does not specifically name all of the impairments that are covered.

ADA TITLE I:
EMPLOYMENT

Title I requires employers with fifteen or more employees to provide qualified individuals with disabilities an equal opportunity to benefit from the full range of employment-related opportunities available to others. For example, it prohibits discrimination in recruitment, hiring, promotions, training, pay, social activities, and other privileges of employment. It restricts questions that can be asked about an applicant's disability before a job offer is made, and it requires that employers make reasonable accommodation to the known physical or mental limitations of otherwise qualified individuals with disabilities, unless it results in undue hardship. Religious entities with fifteen or more employees are covered under title I.

Title I complaints must be filed with the U. S. Equal Employment Opportunity Commission (EEOC) within 180 days of the date of discrimination, or three hundred days if the charge is filed with a designated state or local fair employment practice agency. Individuals may file a lawsuit in federal court only after they receive a "right-to-sue" letter from the EEOC.

Charges of employment discrimination on the basis of disability may be filed at any U.S. Equal Employment Opportunity Commission field office. Field offices are located in fifty cities throughout the U.S. and are listed in most telephone directories under "U.S. Government."

ADA TITLE II:
STATE AND LOCAL GOVERNMENT ACTIVITIES

Title II covers all activities of state and local governments regardless of the government entity's size or receipt of federal funding. Title II requires that state and local governments give people with disabilities an equal opportunity to benefit from all of their programs, services, and activities (e.g. public education, employment, transportation, recreation, health care, social services, courts, voting, and town meetings).

State and local governments are required to follow specific architectural standards in the new construction and alteration of their buildings. They also must relocate programs or otherwise provide access in inaccessible older buildings and communicate effectively with people who have hearing, vision, or speech disabilities. Public entities are not required to take actions that would result in undue financial and administrative burdens. They are required to make reasonable modifications to policies, practices, and procedures where necessary to avoid discrimination, unless they can demonstrate that doing so would fundamentally alter the nature of the service, program, or activity being provided.

Complaints of title II violations may be filed with the Department of Justice within 180 days of the date of discrimination. In certain situations, cases may be referred to a mediation program sponsored by the Department. The Department may bring a lawsuit where it has investigated a matter and has been unable to resolve violations.

Title II may also be enforced through private lawsuits in federal court. It is not necessary to file a complaint with the Department of Justice (DOJ) or any other federal agency, or to receive a "right-to-sue" letter, before going to court.

ADA TITLE II:
PUBLIC TRANSPORTATION

The transportation provisions of title II cover public transportation services, such as city buses and public rail transit (e.g. subways, commuter rails, Amtrak). Public transportation authorities may not discriminate against people with disabilities in the provision of their services. They must comply with requirements for accessibility in newly purchased vehicles, make good faith efforts to purchase or lease accessible used buses, remanufacture buses in an accessible manner, and, unless it would result in an undue burden, provide paratransit where they operate fixed-route bus or rail systems. Paratransit is a service where individuals who are unable to use the regular transit system independently (because of a physical or mental impairment) are picked up and dropped off at their destinations.

ADA TITLE III:
PUBLIC ACCOMMODATIONS

Title III covers businesses and nonprofit service providers that are public accommodations, privately operated entities offering certain types of courses and examinations, privately operated transportation, and commercial facilities. Public accommodations are private entities who own, lease, lease to, or operate facilities such as restaurants, retail stores, hotels, movie theaters, private schools, convention centers, doctors' offices, homeless shelters, transportation depots, zoos, funeral homes, day care centers, and recreation facilities including sports stadiums and fitness clubs. Transportation services provided by private entities are also covered by title III.

Public accommodations must comply with basic nondiscrimination requirements that prohibit exclusion, segregation, and unequal treatment. They also must comply with specific requirements related to architectural standards for new and altered buildings; reasonable modifications to policies, practices, and procedures; effective communication with people with hearing, vision, or speech disabilities; and other access requirements. Additionally, public accommodations must remove barriers in existing buildings where it is easy to do so without much difficulty or expense, given the public accommodation's resources.

Courses and examinations related to professional, educational, or trade-related applications, licensing, certifications, or credentialing must be provided in a place and manner accessible to people with disabilities, or alternative accessible arrangements must be offered.

Commercial facilities, such as factories and warehouses, must comply with the ADA's architectural standards for new construction and alterations.

Complaints of title III violations may be filed with the Department of Justice. In certain situations, cases may be referred to a mediation program sponsored by the Department. The Department is authorized to bring a lawsuit where there is a pattern or practice of discrimination in violation of title III, or where an act of discrimination raises an issue of general public importance. Title III may also be enforced through private lawsuits. It is not necessary to file a complaint with the Department of Justice (or any federal agency), or to receive a "right-to-sue" letter, before going to court.

ADA TITLE IV:
TELECOMMUNICATIONS RELAY SERVICES

Title IV addresses telephone and television access for people with hearing and speech disabilities. It requires common carriers (telephone companies) to establish interstate and intrastate telecommunications relay services (TRS) 24 hours a day, 7 days a week. TRS enables callers with hearing and speech disabilities who use telecommunications devices for the deaf (TDDs), which are also known as teletypewriters (TTYs), and callers who use voice telephones to communicate with each other through a third party communications assistant. The Federal Communications Commission (FCC) has set minimum standards for TRS services. Title IV also requires closed captioning of federally funded public service announcements.

TELECOMMUNICATIONS ACT

Section 255 and Section 251(a)(2) of the Communications Act of 1934, as amended by the Telecommunications Act of 1996, require manufacturers of telecommunications equipment and providers of telecommunications services to ensure that such equipment and services are accessible to and usable by persons with disabilities, if readily achievable. These amendments ensure that people with disabilities will have access to a broad range of products and services such as telephones, cell phones, pagers, call-waiting, and operator services, that were often inaccessible to many users with disabilities.

FAIR HOUSING ACT

The Fair Housing Act, as amended in 1988, prohibits housing discrimination on the basis of race, color, religion, sex, disability, familial status, and national origin. Its coverage includes private housing, housing that receives federal financial assistance, and state and local government housing. It is unlawful to discriminate in any aspect of selling or renting housing or to deny a dwelling to a buyer or renter because of the disability of that individual, an individual associated with the buyer or renter, or an individual who intends to live in the residence. Other covered activities include, for example, financing, zoning practices, new construction design, and advertising.

The Fair Housing Act requires owners of housing facilities to make reasonable exceptions in their policies and operations to afford people with disabilities equal housing opportunities. For example, a landlord with a "no pets" policy may be required to grant an exception to this rule and allow an individual who is blind to keep a guide dog in the residence. The Fair Housing Act also requires landlords to allow tenants with disabilities to make reasonable access-related modifications to their private living space, as well as to common use spaces. (The landlord is not required to pay for the changes.) The Act further requires that new multifamily housing with four or more units be designed and built to allow access for persons with disabilities. This includes accessible common use areas, doors that are wide enough for wheelchairs, kitchens and bathrooms that allow a person using a wheelchair to maneuver, and other adaptable features within the units.

Complaints of Fair Housing Act violations may be filed with the U.S. Department of Housing and Urban Development.

Additionally, the Department of Justice can file cases involving a pattern or practice of discrimination. The Fair Housing Act may also be enforced through private lawsuits.

AIR CARRIER ACCESS ACT

The Air Carrier Access Act prohibits discrimination in air transportation by domestic and foreign air carriers against qualified individuals with physical or mental impairments. It applies only to air carriers that provide regularly scheduled services for hire to the public. Requirements address a wide range of issues including boarding assistance and certain accessibility features in newly built aircraft and new or altered airport facilities. People may enforce rights under the Air Carrier Access Act by filing a complaint with the U.S. Department of Transportation or by bringing a lawsuit in federal court.

VOTING ACCESSIBILITY FOR THE ELDERLY AND HANDICAPPED ACT

The Voting Accessibility for the Elderly and Handicapped Act of 1984 generally requires polling places across the United States to be physically accessible to people with disabilities for federal elections. Where no accessible location is available to serve as a polling place, a political subdivision must provide an alternate means of casting a ballot on the day of the election. This law also requires states to make available registration and voting aids for disabled and elderly voters, including information by telecommunications devices for the deaf (TDDs), which are also known as teletypewriters (TTYs).

NATIONAL VOTER REGISTRATION ACT

The National Voter Registration Act of 1993, also known as the "Motor Voter Act," makes it easier for all Americans to exercise their fundamental right to vote. One of the basic purposes of the Act is to increase the historically low registration rates of minorities and persons with disabilities that have resulted from discrimination. The Motor Voter Act requires all offices of state-funded programs that are primarily engaged in providing services to persons with disabilities to provide all program applicants with voter registration forms, to assist them in completing the forms, and to transmit completed forms to the appropriate state official.

CIVIL RIGHTS OF INSTITUTIONALIZED PERSONS ACT

The Civil Rights of Institutionalized Persons Act (CRIPA) authorizes the U.S. Attorney General to investigate conditions of confinement at state and local government institutions such as prisons, jails, pretrial detention centers, juvenile correctional facilities, publicly operated nursing homes, and institutions for people with psychiatric or developmental disabilities. Its purpose is to allow the Attorney General to uncover and correct widespread deficiencies that seriously jeopardize the health and safety of residents of institutions. The Attorney General does not have authority under CRIPA to investigate isolated incidents or to represent individual institutionalized persons.

The Attorney General may initiate civil law suits where there is reasonable cause to believe that conditions are "egregious or flagrant," that they are subjecting residents to "grievous harm," and that they are part of a "pattern or practice" of resistance to residents' full enjoyment of constitutional or federal rights, including title II of the ADA and section 504 of the Rehabilitation Act.

INDIVIDUALS WITH DISABILITIES EDUCATION ACT

The Individuals with Disabilities Education Act (IDEA) (formerly called PL 94-142 or the Education for all Handicapped Children Act of 1975) requires public schools to make available to all eligible children with disabilities a free appropriate public education in the least restrictive environment appropriate to their individual needs.

IDEA requires public school systems to develop appropriate Individualized Education Programs (IEP's) for each child. The specific special education and related services outlined in each IEP reflect the individualized needs of each student.

IDEA also mandates that particular procedures be followed in the development of the IEP. Each student's IEP must be developed by a team of knowledgeable persons and must be at least reviewed annually. The team includes the child's teacher; the parents, subject to certain limited exceptions; the child, if determined appropriate; an agency representative who is qualified to provide or supervise the provision of special education; and other individuals at the parents' or agency's discretion.

If parents disagree with the proposed IEP, they can request a due process hearing and a review from the state educational agency if applicable in that state. They also can appeal the state agency's decision to state or federal court.

REHABILITATION ACT

The Rehabilitation Act prohibits discrimination on the basis of disability in programs conducted by federal agencies, in programs receiving federal financial assistance, in federal employment, and in the employment practices of federal contractors. The standards for determining employment discrimination under the Rehabilitation Act are the same as those used in title I of the Americans with Disabilities Act.

SECTION 501

Section 501 requires affirmative action and nondiscrimination in employment by federal agencies of the executive branch. To obtain more information or to file a complaint, employees should contact their agency's Equal Employment Opportunity Office.

SECTION 503

Section 503 requires affirmative action and prohibits employment discrimination by federal government contractors and subcontractors with contracts of more than $10,000.

SECTION 504

Section 504 states that "no qualified individual with a disability in the United States shall be excluded from, denied the benefits of, or be subjected to discrimination under" any program or activity that either receives federal financial assistance or is conducted by any executive agency or the United States Postal Service.

Each federal agency has its own set of section 504 regulations that apply to its own programs. Agencies that provide federal financial assistance also have section 504 regulations covering entities that receive federal aid. Requirements common to these regulations include reasonable accommodation for employees with disabilities; program accessibility; effective communication with people who have hearing or vision disabilities; and accessible new construction and alterations. Each agency is responsible for enforcing its own regulations. Section 504 may also be enforced through private lawsuits. It is not necessary to file a complaint with a federal agency or to receive a "right-to-sue" letter before going to court.

For information on how to file 504 complaints with the appropriate agency, contact: U.S. Department of Justice Civil Rights Division.

SECTION 508

Section 508 establishes requirements for electronic and information technology developed, maintained, procured, or used by the federal government. Section 508 requires federal electronic and information technology to be accessible to people with disabilities, including employees and members of the public.

An accessible information technology system is one that can be operated in a variety of ways and does not rely on a single sense or ability of the user. For example, a system that provides output in visual format only may not be accessible to people with visual impairments, and a system that provides output in audio format only may not be accessible to people who are deaf or hard of hearing. Some individuals with disabilities may need accessibility-related software or peripheral devices in order to use systems that comply with Section 508.

ARCHITECTURAL BARRIERS ACT

The Architectural Barriers Act (ABA) requires that buildings and facilities that are designed, constructed, or altered with federal funds, or leased by a federal agency, comply with federal standards for physical accessibility. ABA requirements are limited to architectural standards in new and altered buildings and in newly leased facilities. They do not address the activities conducted in those buildings and facilities. Facilities of the U.S. Postal Service are covered by the ABA.

NOTES

CHAPTER 1

1. "Americans with Disabilities Act Questions and Answers," ADA.gov.
2. Patricia A. Morrissey, *A Primer for Corporate America on Civil Rights for the Disabled* (Virginia: LRP Publications, 1991).
3. "ADA Guide to Small Business," United States Department of Justice, 1995.
4. "ADA Guide to Small Business," DOJ.
5. Marvin Olasky, *Tragedy of American Compassion* (Washington, D.C.: Regnery, 1995).
6. Roy Maynard, "Shape Up or Shut Down," *World*, September 30, 1995.
7. Marvin Olasky, "Home Affront," *World*, April 26, 2003.
8. Edward L. Hudgins, "Handicapping Freedom: The Americans with Disabilities Act," *Regulation*, Vol. 18, No. 2, 1995.
9. Craig E. Richardson and Geoff C. Ziebart, *Strangled by Red Tape: A Heritage Foundation of Horror Stories* (Washington, D.C.: Heritage Books, Inc., 1995).
10. James Bovard, *Lost Rights* (New York: St. Martin's Press, 1994), 187.
11. "Experimental Treatment?" *World*, April 19, 2003.
12. Greg Perry, "The ADA Divides and Conquers," JRNyquist.com, available at http://www.jrnyquist.com/aug27/disabling_america.htm.

CHAPTER 2

1. "Gambling Takes Toll on Individuals, Communities," *Reuters*, November 6, 1998.

2. "Gambling Takes Toll," *USA Today*, November 23, 1998.
3. Roy Maynard, "Shape Up or Shut Down," *World*, September 30, 1995.
4. Maynard, "Shape Up or Shut Down."
5. Maynard, "Shape Up or Shut Down."
6. "The Americans with Disabilities Act," Center for an Accessible Society, available at http://www.accessiblesociety.org/topics/ada/.
7. John Elvin, "Civil Rights—ADA's Good Intentions Have Unintended Consequences," *Insight*, February 21, 2000.
8. *The Diane Rehm Show*, National Public Radio, July 24, 2000.
9. James Bovard, *Lost Rights* (New York: St. Martin's Press, 1994), 186.
10. Larry Elder, "The People's Republic of Santa Monica," Creator's Syndicate, July 13, 2001.
11. James Bovard, "Disability Intentions Astray," *Washington Times*, May 20, 1996.
12. Rendon *v.* Valleycrest Productions, Ltd., 294 F. 3d 1279 (11th Cir. 2002)
13. Bovard, *Lost Rights*, 187-188.
14. Sarah J. McCarthy and Ralph R. Reiland, *Mom & Pop vs. The Dream Busters* (New York: McGraw-Hill Primis, 1999).
15. Jennifer G. Hickey, "Pork and Regulations – Bringing Home the Bacon from the Hill," *Insight*, April 6, 1998.
16. Hickey, "Pork and Regulations."
17. James Bovard, "A Law That Is Disabling Our Courts," *Reader's Digest*, October 1995.
18. Chris Stamper, "Seating Showdown," *World*, December 14, 2002.
19. "Justice Department Sues Major Movie Theater Chain for Failing to Comply with ADA," Department of Justice press release, January 29, 1999.
20. Stamper, "Seating Showdown."
21. Bovard, "Disability Intentions Astray."
22. Bovard, "Disability Intentions Astray."
23. Hickey, "Pork and Regulations."
24. John Elvin, "The New Wave of Regulation," *Insight*, October 26, 1998.
25. *The Diane Rehm Show*, NPR.
26. Sean Paige, "Waste and Abuse," *Insight*, November 13, 2000.
27. "The Americans with Disabilities Act," Center for an Accessible Society, available at http://www.accessiblesociety.org/topics/ada/.

CHAPTER 3

1. "What is Thalidomide?" Thalidomide Victims Association of Canada, available at http://www.thalidomide.ca/en/information/what_is_thalidomide.html.
2. *Bob Enyart Live*, LeSEA Broadcasting Network.
3. Greg Perry, *Managing Rental Properties for Maximum Profit*, 3rd ed. (Roseville, Prima, 2000).
4. Statement from John Mangopoulos, editor of *The Unreported News*, 1995.

CHAPTER 4

1. John Casey, *University of Puget Sound Law Review*, Winter 1994; Llewellyn H. Rockwell, Jr., "What is Disabled?" *The FREE Market*, Ludwig Von Mises Institute, March 1995.
2. John Merline, "Firms Still Facing Gray Areas in Disabilities Act Rules," *Investor's Business Daily*, March 5, 1996.
3. Edward L. Hudgins, "Handicapping Freedom: The Americans with Disabilities Act," *Regulation*, Vol. 18, No. 2, 1995.
4. "Portraying People with Disabilities," Easter Seals Southern California, available at http://www.essc.org/MediaInformation/MediaTips.html.
5. Walter K. Olson, *The Excuse Factory* (New York: Free Press, 1997), 94-95.
6. Olson, 94-95.
7. Joseph Shapiro, *No Pity: People with Disabilities Forging a New Civil Rights Movement*, (New York: Random House/Three Rivers, 1993).
8. Olson, 95.
9. "Publications of S.W. Hawking," November 26, 2002, available at http://www.hawking.org.uk/pdf/pub.pdf.
10. Hudgins, "Handicapping Freedom."
11. Frederic Bastiat, *The Law* (New York: Foundation for Economic Education, 1995).
12. Llewellyn H. Rockwell, "The ADA Racket," Ludwig von Mises Institute, May 16, 2003.
13. "Non-disabled Employee Wins ADA Case," FairMeasures.com, available at http://www.fairmeasures.com/whatsnew/archive/spring96/new01.html.
14. "Non-disabled Employee Wins ADA Case," FairMeasures.com.
15. Trevor Armbrister, "A Good Law Gone Bad," *Reader's Digest*, May 1998.

16. Gilbert F. Casellas, "Forget Sympathy, We're Talking Justice," *Wall Street Journal*, July 14, 1995.
17. Hudgins, "Handicapping Freedom."
18. James Bovard, "The ADA: Attorney's Dreams Answered," The Future of Freedom Foundation, May, 1996.
19. Llewellyn H. Rockwell, Jr., "The New Welfare Bums," LewRockwell.com, September 6, 2002.
20. *The Diane Rehm Show*, National Public Radio, July 24, 2000.
21. Stephen Cooper, "Benefits from ADA Law Come at a Cost to Employers, Experts Say," *Business Owner's Tookit*, December 7, 1998, available at http://www.toolkit.cch.com/columns/people/024adacosts.asp.
22. Larry Elder, "The People's Republic of Santa Monica," Creator's Syndicate, July 13, 2001.
23. Charles T. Canady, "The ADA Notification Act," Subcommittee on the Constitution, Rayburn House Office Building, Hearing on H.R. 3590, May 18, 2000.
24. Joseph R. Fields, "Letter to Chairman Charles T. Canady regarding the ADA Notification Act," May 16, 2000.
25. Olson, 96-97.
26. Olson, 98, 101.
27. *The Diane Rehm Show*, NPR.

CHAPTER 5

1. Edward L. Hudgins, "Handicapping Freedom: The Americans with Disabilities Act," *Regulation*, Vol. 18, No. 2, 1995.
2. Llewellyn H. Rockwell, Jr., "ADA Success? At What?" LewRockwell.com, August 3, 2001.
3. "Fat Man Sues McDonald's Over Non-Hire," Associated Press, April 18, 2003.
4. Myles Kantor, "Give 'Em Hell, Harry," LewRockwell.com, September 23, 2000.
5. *Bob Enyart*, KGOV Radio.
6. "Disability Right Attorney Accused of Having Inaccessible Office," Overlawyered.com, April 2002.
7. "Disability Rights Attorney Accused of Having Inaccessible Office," *Contra Costa Times*, April 23, 2002, available at http://www.bayarea.com/mld/cctimes/news/breaking_news/3124059.htm.
8. "Disability Rights Attorney Accused of Having Inaccessible Office," *Contra Costa Times*.
9. Joy Lanzendorfer, "George Louie wants California safe for the

disabled, and he wants it now," *North Bay Bohemian*, December 26, 2002.

10. Lanzendorfer, "George Louie wants California Safe for the disabled."

11. Lanzendorfer, "George Louie wants California Safe for the disabled."

12. "ADA Guide for Small Business," U.S. Department of Justice, Civil Rights Division, n.d.

13. "ADA Guide for Small Business," DOJ.

14. Jeff Elkins, "Fore!," LewRockwell.com, June 4, 2001.

15. Shannon P. Duffy, "Jury Awards Woman with Crohn's Disease $1.5 Million in ADA Case," Overlawyered.com, June 2000.

16. Lanzendorfer, "George Louie wants California Safe for the disabled."

17. "ADA's Busiest Complaint-Filer," Overlawyered.com, July 2001.

18. *The Diane Rehm Show*, National Public Radio, July 24, 2000.

19. Hudgins, "Handicapping Freedom."

20. Hudgins, "Handicapping Freedom."

21. Llewellyn H. Rockwell, Jr., "What is Disabled?" *The FREE Market*, Ludwig Von Mises Institute, March, 1995.

22. For more info, visit AAPD.com.

23. "October 15, 2003, Designated as Disability Mentoring Day by Labor Secretary Chao," Shepherd Center, July 21, 2003, available at http://www.shepherd.org/shepherdhomepage.nsf/0/74d6de5453fdcfbf8525699f0052dec9.

24. Walter K. Olson, *The Excuse Factory* (New York: Free Press, 1997), 86.

25. Olson, 90.

26. Olson, 91.

27. Nadine Heintz, "Disability's Deep Costs," *Inc. Magazine*, June 2003.

CHAPTER 6

1. *Bob Enyart Live*, World Harvest Network, 1998.

2. *Hate Crime in Idaho*, Idaho state government publication, 2001.

3. Llewellyn H. Rockwell, "ADA Success? At What?" LewRockwell.com, August 3, 2001.

4. Rockwell, "ADA Success? At What?"

5. Kathi Wolfe, "Bashing the Disabled: The New Hate Crime," *The Progressive*, date unknown.

6. Mari Carlin Dart, "The Resurrection of Justin Dart, Jr., A Quest for Truth and Love," *Ability Magazine*, available at http://www.ability-magazine.com/carroll_dart.html

7. Dart, "The Resurrection of Justin Dart, Jr."
8. "What About at Christmas?" TongueTied.us, October 11, 2002, available at http://www.tonguetied.us/archives/000018.php.
9. "What About at Christmas?" TongueTied.us.
10. Diane Ravitch, *The Language Police*, (New York: Knopf, 2003).
11. Ravitch, *The Language Police*.
12. John Mangopoulos, *The Un-Reported News*, February 28, 1997.
13. *"Ambiguous Bathrooms,"* TongueTied.us, January 29, 2003, available at http://www.tonguetied.us/archives/000247.php.
14. Nick Manetto, "State Court: Transsexuals Protected under Law, The Times," *New Jersey Times*, July 4, 2001.
15. Nick Manetto, "State Court: Transsexuals Protected under Law."
16. C. Barillas, "Justice Dept Sides with HIV+ Woman in ADA Case," DataLounge.com, February 12, 1998.
17. Gerald D. Skoning, "Legal Weirdness at Work," *The National Law Journal*, March 26, 2003.
18. James Bovard, "A Law That Is Disabling Our Courts," *Reader's Digest*, October 1995.
19. Spina Bifida Association of America, SBAA.org.
20. Steven W. Mosher, "The Repackaging of Margaret Sanger," *Wall Street Journal*, May 5, 1997.
21. Hillary Rodham Clinton, "Remarks for the World Health Organization Forum on Women and Health Security," U.N. Summit, September 5, 1995.
22. "Planned Parenthood Federation of America," available at http://member.plannedparenthood.org/site/PageServer?pagename=1990_1995.
23. Mosher, "The Repackaging of Margaret Sanger."
24. Reggie White, "Abortion and the African-American: Is it Genocide?" North Baton Rouge Women's Help Center available at http://www.pregnancycenters.org/batonrouge/abortionafican.html.
25. White, "Abortion and the African-American."
26. White, "Abortion and the African-American."
27. Mosher, "The Repackaging of Margaret Sanger."
28. "The Fetus May Be Deformed," Abortiontv.com, available at http://www.abortiontv.com/TheFetusMay.htm.
29. David C. Reardon, Ph.D, "March of Dimes Ignores Abortion-Premature Birth Link," *Christian Life Resources*, October 2, 2003.
30. David C. Reardon, Ph.D, "March of Dimes Ignores Abortion-Premature Birth Link."

31. March of Dimes, MoDimes.org.
32. Trevor Armrister, "A Good Law Gone Bad," *Reader's Digest*, May 1998.
33. *Fragrance Zones*, www.tonguetied.us, April 28, 2003.
34. Skoning, "Legal Weirdness at Work."

CHAPTER 7
1. Phone conversation with Bettye Perry and the former teacher, Tulsa, Oklahoma, May 2003.
2. Robert Holland, "Disabled Children Need a Better IDEA," *School Reform News*, September 2002.
3. Holland, "Disabled Children Need a Better IDEA."
4. Arthur B. Robinson, *Access to Energy*, May 2003, page 4.
5. Holland, "Disabled Children Need a Better IDEA."
6. Holland, "Disabled Children Need a Better IDEA."
7. Stephen Goode, "Special Education – Classroom Disruption," *Insight*, 2002.
8. Goode, "Special Education."
9. Goode, "Special Education."
10. Carolyn Ito, "IDEA Reauthorization," Training and Technical Assistance Center at the College of William and Mary, 1997.
11. Goode, "Special Education."
12. John Berlau, "Special Education for Everybody?" *Insight*, date unknown.
13. Linda Schrock Taylor, "No Exit: The 'Black Hole' of Special Education," Alliance for the Separation of School & State, SepSchool.org, December 5, 2002.
14. Linda Schrock Taylor, "No Exit: Statistics," Alliance for the Separation of School & State, SepSchool.org, January 4, 2003.
15. Taylor, "No Exit: Statistics."
16. Brandon Dutcher, "Educators Respond with Higher Doses of Political Correctness and Ritalin," *The Education Liberator*, www.sepschools.org, February 23, 1996.
17. Berlau, "Special Education for Everybody?"
18. Berlau, "Special Education for Everybody?"
19. Peter R. Breggin, *Talking Back to Ritalin: What Doctors Aren't Telling You About Stimulants for Children* (Monroe: Common Courage Press, 1998).
20. "History of the Able Child," Ablechild.org, available at http://ablechild.org/history.htm.
21. Gene Warner, "A Crusade for Shaina," *Buffalo News*, May 21, 2003.

22. Gary North, "William Bennett: The Pusher," LewRockwell.com, May 12, 2003.

23. Karen Thomas, "Parents Pressured to Put Kids on Ritalin," *USA Today*, August 8, 2000.

24. Thomas, "Parents Pressured to Put Kids on Ritalin."

25. Cathy Cuthbert, "The Rise of the American Empire," Alliance for the Separation of School & State, SepSchool.org, date unknown.

26. Cathy Duffy, "The Voucher Poses Problems for Both Traditional Private Schools and Homeschools," Alliance for the Separation of School & State, SepSchool.org, October 21, 2000.

27. John Flanagan, "The ADA and Catholic School," LewRockwell. com, January 29, 2001.

28. Alliance for the Separation of School and State, SepSchool.org.

29. Rich Jefferson, "Children with Learning Disabilities Do Better in Home Schools than in Special Needs Programs at Public Schools," Home School Legal Defense Association, HSLDA.org, September 4, 1997.

30. RobinsonCurriculum.com.

CHAPTER 8

1. James Bovard, *Freedom in Chains* (New York: Palgrave Macmillan, 2000).

2. Edward L. Hudgins, "Handicapping Freedom," *Regulation*, Vol. 18, No. 2, 1995.

3. Jonathan Steven Greenhouse, "Lifetime Affliction Leads to a U.S. Bias Suit," *New York Times*, March 30, 2003.

4. McDonald's corporate pamphlet, 2003.

5. Greg Perry, *Managing Rental Properties for Maximum Profit*, 3rd ed. (Prima: Roseville, 2000).

6. "Recommended Language or Inclusion in New and Renewed Lease Agreements," Minneapolis Public Schools, available at http://www.mpls.k12.mn.us.

7. "On the Job: Local Businesses to Mentor Individuals with Disabilities," *Wichita State University News Digest*, October 11, 2002.

8. Andy Humbles, "Members of Tau Kappa Epsilon Assist Future Eagle Scout," *Tennessean*, December 5, 2002.

9. Greater New York Councils, Boy Scouts of America, BSA-GNYC.org.

10. Holly Edwards, "Cub Scout Crawls Grave to Grave, Honoring the Dead," *Tennessean*, May 23, 2003.
11. "The Building Blocks of Scouting, Scouts with Special Needs," Boy Scouts of America, available at http://www.scouting.org/boyscouts/resources/34307/specneeds.html.
12. "Jim Stovall Biography," NTN Narrative Television Network, available at http://www.narrativetv.com/jimbio.htm.
13. LittleLightHouse.org.
14. "National Service Available for Sportsmen with Physical Disabilities," *Alliance Voice*, September 1995.
15. "Women of NRA-Beeman Tour Make Shooting Sports History," *Shooting Sports*, January/February 2003.

CHAPTER 9

1. "Labor Department Hosts UK-US Seminar Seeking Exchange of Ideas on Improving Employment Opportunities for People with Disabilities," *AAPD News*, May, 2003.
2. "S. African Wins Payout After Prison HIV Infection," *Reuters*, February 12, 2003.
3. "French Debate Killing Disabled People," NewsMax.com, December 17, 2001.
4. "French Debate Killing Disabled People," NewsMax.com.
5. *Bob Enyart Live*, World Harvest Network, 1997.
6. "Name Nazis," *World*, May 17, 2003.
7. "Protest to Assert Rights," *Labour File Journal*, March 2003.
8. "Protest to Assert Rights," *Labour File Journal*.
9. "Protest to Assert Rights," *Labour File Journal*.
10. Steven Yates, "From Carroll Quigley to the UN Millennium Summit: Thoughts on the New World Order," LewRockwell.com, September 9, 2000.
11. Yates, "From Carroll Quigley to the UN Millennium Summit."
12. Yates, "From Carroll Quigley to the UN Millennium Summit."
13. "United Nations Enable," UN.org, available at http://www.un.org/esa/socdev/enable/.
14. "Airport Forces Girl to Remove Fake Limb," WND.com, April 23, 2003.
15. "Airport Forces Girl to Remove Fake Limb," WND.com.
16. "Airport Forces Girl to Remove Fake Limb," WND.com.

CHAPTER 10

1. "New Freedom Initiative," HHS.gov, available at http://www.hhs.gov/newfreedom/.

2. Larry Elder, "The People's Republic of Santa Monica," Creator's Syndicate, July 13, 2001.

3. Elder, "The People's Republic of Santa Monica."

4. John Schaub, *Gary North's Remnant Review*, May 16, 2003.

5. "Visitability Bill Introduced in Congress," The Center for An Accessible Society, June 10, 2003.

6. "Sidewalks Are Covered By Disabilities Act, Says White House Attorney," The Center for an Accessible Society, June 10, 2003.

7. "Web Accessibility Initiative (WAI)," World Wide Web Consortium, available at http://www.w3.org.

8. James L. Gattuso, "Internet-1, Lawyers-0: The ADA in Cyberspace," *InPrint@CEI*, CEI.org, October 25, 2002.

9. Gattuso, "Internet-1, Lawyers-0."

10. Gattuso, "Internet-1, Lawyers-0."

11. Stephen Hawking, "A Brief History of Mine," Hawking.org.

12. Troy Justesen, "President's Executive Memorandum on Assistive Technology Mobility Devices," American Association of People with Disabilities, May 2003.

13. "A Campaign to Protect the Civil Rights of People with Disabilities," Mission Statement, ADA Watch, available ay http://www.adawatch.org/mission.asp.

14. "Watch the ADA Notification Act," ADA Watch, available at http://www.adawatch.org.

15. "The Americans with Disabilities Act," The Center for an Accessible Society, available at http://www.accessiblesociety.org/topics/ada/.

INDEX

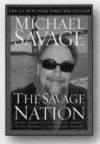

The Savage Nation

Savage's original electrifying book warns that our country is losing its identity and becoming a victim of political correctness, unmonitored immigration, and socialistic ideals. Michael Savage, whose program is the fourth-largest radio talk show and is heard on more than three hundred stations coast-to-coast, uses bold, biting, and hilarious straight talk in this national bestseller to aim at the sacred cows of our ever-eroding culture and wages a war against the "group of psychopaths" known as PETA, the ACLU, and the liberal media. 0-7852-6353-5

Breach of Trust

This is Tom Coburn's gripping story of how he and other Republican revolutionaries took Congress by storm as part of the historic "Class of '94," tried to wrest control from the hands of career politicians and push forward with legislation that would dramatically limit the size and scope of government, but found that Washington was unwilling to change. With many behind-the-scenes details of Congress backbiting and bungles, Coburn sheds new light on the rampant misuse of government funds, pork barrel shenanigans, shameless attempts to "buy" votes, and the unbelievable ways the system often turns politicians against their own constituents. 0-7852-6271-7

Journalistic Fraud

For over a hundred years, the *New York Times* has purported to present straight news and hard facts. But, as Bob Kohn shows in this book, the founders' original vision has been hijacked, and today, instead of straight news, readers are given mere editorial under the pretense of objective journalism. Kohn, a lifelong reader of the *Times*, shows point-by-point the methods by which the *Times'* mission has been subverted by the present management and how such fraudulence directly corrupts hundreds of news agencies around the world. 0-7852-6104-4

Scam

In this scorching exposé of today's most outspoken civil-rights leaders, Rev. Jesse Lee Peterson lays bare the black community's corrupt leadership and encourages black Americans to shake off the stranglehold of these so-called leaders and take control of a future full of hope and promise. With fiery conviction, Peterson courageously takes aim at the biggest names—Jesse Jackson, Louis Farrakhan, Al Sharpton, and Maxine Waters, among others—claiming that they are nothing more than "scam artists" profiting off the hatred and disorder they foster in the black community. **0-7852-6331-4**

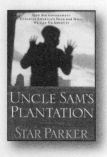

Uncle Sam's Plantation

Star Parker's book is an incisive look at how government manipulates, controls, and ultimately devastates the lives of the poor—and what we as Americans must do to stop it. Argued with fresh perspective, hard-won intelligence, and the fierce yet compassionate heart of a woman who has been chewed up and spit out by our country's ruthless welfare system, this book lays out a far more constructive, empowering plan to combat poverty—one that encourages faith, individual responsibility, and personalized treatment. **0-7852-6219-9**

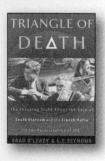

Triangle of Death

This is the startling new book that proves President John F. Kennedy was killed as a result of a massive conspiracy between the CIA-controlled government of South Vietnam, the French global heroin syndicate, and the New Orleans Mafia. Painstakingly researched with details of a first-time-ever reenactment at Dealey Plaza, an exclusive new interview with one of the assassination's primary players, and federal documents that have only recently been declassified, this book builds a monumental case for conspiracy that is both shocking and utterly convincing. **0-7852-6153-2**

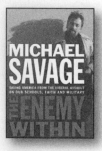

The Enemy Within

Talk radio sensation and *New York Times* best-selling author Michael Savage again goes for the jugular in this latest brash, incendiary attack on the corrosive effects of liberalism on our culture. Where *The Savage Nation* was a grab bag of rants and ravings, this book focuses squarely on the dangers assailing the cornerstones of American life, pointing out how liberal propaganda and agendas are seeping into our churches, our schools, even our families. Bold, sometimes angry, often uproarious, and always controversial, this book is pure no-holds-barred Michael Savage, one of the strongest, most original voices in America today. **0-7852-6102-8**

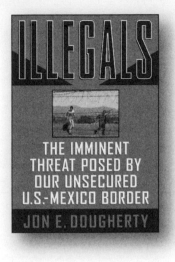

Hand of Providence

This book by Mary Beth Brown explores the life and personality of Ronald Reagan by focusing on his deep-felt Christian beliefs and showing how faith guided him along his distinguished career and led him to his unprecedented success. With the support of Ronald Reagan's own words and writings and firsthand interviews of Ronald Reagan's family, friends, and co-workers, Brown weaves a magnificent story of Reagan's strong devotion to God that will not only inspire Christians to enter public service and allow their faith to motivate all their actions but also help point others to the cross of Jesus Christ—a cause that was near and dear to President Reagan's heart.

0-7852-6053-6

362.1
PER

12/